Gardening for Florida's Butterflies

Pamela F. Traas

A Great Outdoors Book

Great Outdoors Publishing Company
St. Petersburg, Florida

Published by: Great Outdoors Publishing Company
                 4747 28th Street North
                 St. Petersburg, FL 33714
                 (727)525-6609
                 www.floridabooks.com

                 Publisher's Cataloging-in-Publication Data
                    (Provided by Quality Books, Inc.)

Traas, Pamela F.
    Gardening for Florida's butterflies / Pamela F. Traas. -- 2nd ed.
    p. cm.
    Includes bibliographical references and index.
    LCCN: 2001095129
    ISBN: 0-8200-0420-0

    1. Butterflies--Florida. 2. Butterfly gardening--Florida. I. Title.

QL551.F6T73 2001   595.78'9'09759
                                           QBI01-201152

            Manufactured in the United States of America

Dedication

To Donald, my strength, my soul-mate and the love of my life,
Our daughter, a miracle named Natasha and
For my mom, Marylyn (1928–1994)
who was beauty, light, music and laughter
I shall miss and love you forever.

Acknowledgments

I would like to thank the Safety Harbor Elementary PTA, which by asking me to plant a butterfly garden opened up a learning experience that hasn't ended; Craig Huegel, for his book *Butterfly Gardening with Florida's Native Plants,* that inspired me to want to know more about the connection between our butterflies and the plants that support them; Katy Roberts for sharing both her "wild" yard and some growing tips; All the photographers who contributed their work, because I need to see a picture to understand; All the friends of Bill W. and Dr. Bob, especially The Oldsmar Group that has been my spiritual lifeline; My family, Cathy, Bonnie, Rusty, Julie, Dan, Mary, Pops and Margie for all the love and encouragement they gave me. Finally, I'll be forever grateful to Jan Allyn, my publisher and friend for her patience, vision, and motivation, her mom, Joyce Allyn for spoiling us all with homemade lunch on Fridays, and Chris Kelly, for his wicked sense of humor.

Photo Credits

CONTENTS

INTRODUCTION

Butterflies long have been a bridge to the natural world, taking one away from the stress of everyday life. Who isn't captivated by their brilliant colors and languid flight? Who hasn't welcomed a pause from our hurry-up world to watch as a butterfly floats leisurely by? Butterflies seem magical—By inviting them to our gardens we can make ourselves part of their world.

A simple request from the PTA at my daughter's school for campus beautification led to my being asked to install a butterfly garden there. I couldn't wait to get started on my first butterfly haven. The excitement of the children only increased my enthusiasm for the project.

This initial foray into butterfly gardening was begun with more enthusiasm than planning. I bought and planted a huge mish-mash of plants. Although the new garden was beautiful and proved educational, it could have been even better. Although I got lucky in choosing some plants, others were not the favorite nurseries of the winged visitors I had hoped to attract. Installing the school's garden taught me that in order to plant a garden for Florida's butterflies I needed to know more about the plants that support them. To learn more, I joined my local chapter of the Florida Native Plant Society.

© ROGER HAMMER

Giant Swallowtail *(Heraclides cresphontes)* on pentas *(Pentas lanceolata)*

I also began to read every book on butterflies that I could get my hands on, and I visited many butterfly houses. I soon learned what every successful butterfly gardener knows: butterflies are a discriminating lot. Downright picky, in fact! Most species of butterflies will lay their eggs on only a few different kinds of plants, with some accepting only a single species. Adult butterflies may flit from flower to flower, supping from a veritable smorgasbord of nectar, but females will lay their precious eggs only on certain plants—those that Mother Nature has decreed are suitable for that particular species of butterfly. These are the "larval plants" for that species, so called because the caterpillars—the butterfly's larvae—feed on them. Larval plants are also sometimes called "host plants." I learned that if you are interested in attracting and/or raising a certain kind of butterfly, you must find out which larval foods it requires and plant as many of those as space will allow, for it is on the larval food that you will find butterfly eggs and caterpillars.

This book contains information about many—but by no means all—of Florida's butterflies, the nectar plants that attract them, and the larval plants that support them. Depending on how much room you have, what kind of soil and drainage are prevalent, and where you live, some plants will be better suited for your needs than others. Most flowering plants provide some nectar for adult butterflies, but some plants are unusually attractive to them. This may be because their nectar is easily accessible due to the size and shape of the flower, or because the plants are marked with ultraviolet colors that only butterflies can see, alerting them that nectar is especially abundant. The nectar plants described in this book were chosen for these attributes, and because they are available at nurseries. Some may be easier to find than others. There are many other nectar plants that are not included. The best way to find out if a plant is a good butterfly attractor is to try it in your garden. Experiment, learn, and share your knowledge with other gardeners.

Although I have included some cultivated and exotic plants in the following pages, the rare and simple beauty of Florida's native wildflowers have stolen my heart. Neither garish nor obtrusive, they linger unnoticed in the background of the landscape; then, unexpectedly, they burst forth with blossoms, transforming a mundane piece of ground into a carpet of color and life. I encourage you to incorporate Florida native plants in your garden plan, as they are easy to grow and require very little maintenance once established.

Some of Florida's butterflies are better adapted to urban life than others. These yard-friendly fellows are the ones you're most likely to see in your neighborhood, and these are the butterflies included in this book.

We who treasure these living jewels also must become aware of the dwindling habitat of Florida's butterflies. Caught in an onslaught of development and harmed by overuse of chemicals, they are seen less frequently. Too often I arrive at one of my favorite butterfly haunts only to find it replaced by a construction site, as nature yields for yet another building or road. Along Florida highways, mowing machines relentlessly gobble up the plants that grow in ditches and along roadsides, so important for feeding butterflies and their caterpillars.

Instead of bemoaning the unhappy fate of butterflies, come join the growing number of dedicated folks who have wisely taken a different approach. In their own backyards they create new habitat to replace what is being destroyed. Moreover, the butterfly gardens they install at schools, libraries, churches, nursing homes and other public places provide beauty and pleasure to those who pass by.

I hope that this book will simplify butterfly gardening by helping you to identify many of Florida's common garden butterflies, and sharing what I've learned about how to grow the plants that provide food for them. Butterflies are wonderful creatures that you can easily attract by providing for their needs. As pollinators, they help to propagate the beautiful flowers we grow. In our hectic world, it is good to pause and drink in the tranquility of a butterfly sinking softly into a cloud of flowers.

Attracting Butterflies to Your Yard

To create a habitat that will attract these colorful creatures, there are three things you must provide: sunlight, food and cover. Butterflies need warmth, and sunshine provides it. Although you will attract a few strays that will stop to nectar, if you want to experience the entire life cycle of butterflies and keep them coming back to your yard, you must provide food for both caterpillars and adults. Well-placed shrubbery is important to provide places for butterflies to rest and hide from predators.

Butterflies are "solar-powered fliers," so it's important to place some of your butterfly plants where they will receive at least four to six hours of sun a day. Butterflies are cold-blooded and require warmth to fly, mate and reproduce. They use their wings and bodies as solar collectors, which is why we often see them basking in the sunshine.

Planting colorful nectar flowers will almost guarantee butterflies will visit your garden. Different colors seem to attract the attention of different species. Which colors are best is debatable, but from personal experience I have found that yellow, lavender and red attract plenty of butterflies to my garden. And although I read in a butterfly newsletter that a gentleman in the northeast U.S. attracted butterflies with plastic pink flamingos (just another reason to own these wonderful testaments to tackiness), the purpose of colorful flowers is to provide nectar, food for the adult butterflies. This nectar provides the energy the adults require to live in the form of proteins and sugar.

Including larval food plants in your garden is very desirable. Butterflies are very specific and will deposit their eggs only on a very few plants, these usually in the same family. Plants that feed caterpillars are called "host plants" or "larval food plants." The eggs are usually placed on the tips or leaves of the new growth, and the young caterpillars hatch to a veritable feast. After all, their only job is to eat, grow huge, and prepare to change. You will know that you've been successful in attracting a certain species by the disappearance of its host plant. Don't worry about damage to these plants, most are built to withstand the intense munching and will grow back rapidly.

I once happened upon a group of tiger swallowtails engaged in a behavior called "puddling." A dozen butterflies gathered around a small patch of mud. At

the time, I was mesmerized by the size of their group and by the fact that not one of them budged when I came near. I later learned that butterflies (especially males) puddle to gather moisture from mud or sand, absorbing salts and minerals and from it. Scientists believe that these nutrients are used in reproduction. You can provide a moist spot for puddling by sinking a small dish into the soil, then filling it with wet sand. Replenish it with water when it dries.

Butterflies need cover just as birds and other animals do. You can provide it by planting shrubs and small trees on the periphery of your garden, preferably evergreen ones that will allow butterflies a place to escape from wind, rain and predators. Some butterflies also enjoy perching to survey their territory for mates or intruders. A few flat rocks placed in sunny spots throughout the garden will serve as perching or basking places. A complete habitat that will attract butterflies and fill their needs should have sun and trees, water and shrubs, grasses and wildflowers.

As important as what you do in your garden is what you don't do. Pesticides from your lawn (or even drifting from your neighbor's yard) can kill both caterpillars and butterflies. Don't use them. Learn to appreciate a less manicured garden, and both butterflies and the environment will benefit. People who learn about and adopt landscape practices that are harmonious with nature will be rewarded with gardens bursting with life.

Raising Butterflies

B eing able to observe every stage in a butterfly's life cycle is perhaps the most fascinating aspect of butterfly gardening. Butterflies—members of the order Lepidoptera—have four distinct stages, which you may remember from third grade science class: egg, caterpillar (or larva), pupa (or chrysalis) and adult. However, no science book can adequately capture the magic of watching, close up, as a living, brightly-colored creature emerges from a tiny, wrinkled capsule and flutters away. It's a miracle that captivates the child in us all. Judging from the huge number of butterfly gardens popping up in schoolyards everywhere, we can assume thousands of children are experiencing the magic of metamorphosis firsthand. What a great learning experience!

Let's assume that you have decided to raise a particular species of butterfly. You have researched and planted the larval food plants that you know it prefers, and you have seen adult butterflies hovering nearby. It is time to go on an egg hunt! A magnifying glass will help, as butterfly eggs are very tiny. They range in color from pearl to brown, or some-times yellow or green, depending on the species. Their shape may be perfectly round or almost cylindrical. Some butterflies lay eggs singly, while other species lay large clus-ters of eggs. Look for them on new plant growth and on the underside of leaves. When you find an egg, protect it by tying a piece of light-colored, fine mesh (ask for "tulle" at

Gulf fritillary egg

the fabric store) around the area loosely, using a twist tie to secure each end. This will protect the egg from lizards, spiders, wasps, ants and other predators. It will also mark the area to help you locate the egg later, in order to observe its progress. Watch eggs carefully; most caterpillars hatch within a week to ten days. When a caterpillar is about to emerge, the egg turns translucent and you will be able to see the tiny creature inside. After it breaks free of the egg, the caterpillar usually eats the remaining shell, which is rich in protein.

When the caterpillar has grown to about one-quarter of an inch long, you may choose to snip off the part of the plant on which it is feeding and place the caterpillar and its leaf in a rearing box to more easily observe its progress. (You may also leave the caterpillar on the plant inside its mesh "house," but you can see it better in a rearing box.) There are many commercial varieties of caterpillar rearing boxes. Some are made of screen with convenient zippers for access. Some are box shaped, others shaped like pyramids. You can also construct your own rearing box, as I did. I used an old 10-gallon fish tank, covering the top with mesh attached by strips of Velcro. An extra large jar also works well. Use mesh to cover the opening, not the original lid, so that the caterpillars can get fresh air. Your rearing box should be big enough to hold plenty of fresh larval food, but not so large that the caterpillars can get lost among the foliage. I have been more successful raising caterpillars outdoors than in an artificial, air conditioned, indoor environment. Your rearing box should, however, be kept in a sheltered area out of the rain or other bad weather. If you use a glass enclosure, you should also place it out of direct sunlight to prevent it from getting too warm inside. Take care that the inside of the box stays dry, and every day or two remove any caterpillar droppings. If caterpillars come in contact with them, they may sicken and die.

Now you can watch your caterpillars do what they do best—eat. After all, that's a caterpillar's sole purpose. Imagine doing nothing all day except dining on your favorite food, then taking a long nap and waking up beautiful! Some butterflies not only wake up beautiful, but are also fully equipped to ward off enemies. During caterpillar-hood, certain species (such as the milkweed, passionvine, and pipevine caterpillars) store toxin from the plants they eat in their bodies. This toxin renders them distasteful to their predators, not only as caterpillars, but as butterflies, too.

© DONALD TRAAS

Gulf fritillary eggs and caterpillars

As caterpillars eat, they grow. Because they grow more rapidly than their non-stretchable skin allows, every few days they have to shed it. The periods between shedding are called "instars." A caterpillar may go through as many as five instars. Some species change dramatically in color with each shedding. For instance, the zebra swallowtail caterpillar begins life with black and yellow stripes, but ends up with light green and yellow stripes!

After a week or two, the greedy, plump characters in your rearing box will ready themselves to shed their skin for the last time. You will know that this is about to happen when you observe that the caterpillars have (finally!) stopped eating and have begun to wander about restlessly. They are looking for just the right "hangout" to begin the pupa stage, when they are most vulnerable. Once a caterpillar has finally chosen a site, it attaches itself firmly to the spot. Some kinds of caterpillars hang upside down in a "J" shape, stuck by the tail with silk either to the top of the rearing box or to a twig. Others hang nearly parallel to a twig by sticking their tails to it, then lassoing themselves around the middle with another silk strand for balance. After that, the caterpillar makes a final, impressive shrug, causing the last of its skin to drop to the ground. The outer covering of the caterpillar—now a pupa—then starts to harden. Some pupae look like dried-up leaves. Others are exactly the same color as their larval food plant or the twig they are suspended from, a helpful camouflage. Still others sport brilliant markings, warning predators that they are extremely distasteful and are therefore best left alone. In warm weather the pupa stage lasts a week or two. If the air is cold, it may last longer, even all winter. (Many butterflies can hibernate in winter, in whatever stage they happen to be in. In general, cold weather tends to lengthen the time spent in egg, caterpillar and pupa stages, and warm weather tends to shorten it.)

The last stage of a butterfly's life is the adult. Just before the adult emerges, the outer skins of some pupae turn translucent, making the colorful butterfly inside visible. The pupa case splits open and the adult pulls itself out. Because the new butterfly's wings are wet, soft and limp, it cannot fly. It must first pump fluid into its wings to give them strength and stiffness. Most butterflies rest for a few hours before flying away. This is a good time to take photographs. Not only is the butterfly relatively immobile, its colors are fresh and bright and its wings are untattered. However, as soon as a newly-emerged butterfly in your rearing tank can fly, you should release it so that it doesn't injure itself fluttering in a small space. Often, when I've released a butterfly, I look more closely at the visitors to my yard for the next few days, wondering if I know them. But that only lasts a short while, then I'm off collecting another caterpillar or trying to figure out how to entice another species of butterfly into my garden.

Butterfly gardens encourage us to relax into the role of observer, so place plants throughout your landscape where they can be seen easily most of the time. Then spend some time loitering nearby, discovering which butterflies frequent your area. Plant your garden to welcome them and you will realize the many rewards of gardening for Florida's butterflies. Whether you have space only for a window box, or enough room to plant a whole meadow, few types of gardening will bring you as much pleasure as butterfly gardening.

Definitions of Terms Used in this Book

Terms used in the butterfly and plant profiles which follow are described and clarified below.

Butterflies:

Name: *Common and scientific names are given. (Nomenclature conforms to the North American Butterfly Association species list published in June 2001.)*

Family: *The group a specific butterfly is placed in, for purposes of scientific classification.*

Wingspan: *Approximate size from wingtip to wingtip, in inches.*

Florida Range: *The area of Florida in which this butterfly is most commonly observed.*

Season of Flight: *The time of year the butterfly is most active, and therefore most often observed.*

Preferred Habitat: *The kind of surroundings in which the butterfly is most often observed.*

Adult Life Expectancy: *Approximate time spent as an adult butterfly.*

Larval Foods: *Plants that the caterpillars consume.*

Plants:

Name: *Common and scientific names are given. Some species may have more than one common name; generally only the one most frequently used is given. Scientific names are given as genus and species. In some cases, "spp." is used to indicate that the information provided applies to more than one species within the same genus.*

Family: *Group a specific plant is placed in, for purposes of scientific classification.*

Plant Type:

  Annual—Germinates, blooms, goes to seed and dies within one year.

  Biennial—Germinates, blooms, goes to seed and dies within two years.

  Perennial—Returns for three years or more from the same root stock.

  Evergreen—A plant that keeps its leaves during all seasons.

  Herbaceous—A plant without woody stems that usually dies back to the ground each year.

  Shrub—A bushy, woody plant that has multiple stems.

  Tree— A plant that has one trunk with many branches.

  Groundcover—A spreading, low-growing plant.

  Wildflower—A flowering plant that grows without cultivation.

  Aquatic—A plant that grows in or on water.

Florida Zones: *The Florida zones listed are where a plant is capable of growing, and may extend beyond its natural range (see map at right)*

Mature Size: *Approximate maximum height and width of a fully-grown plant, useful for determining plant spacing.*

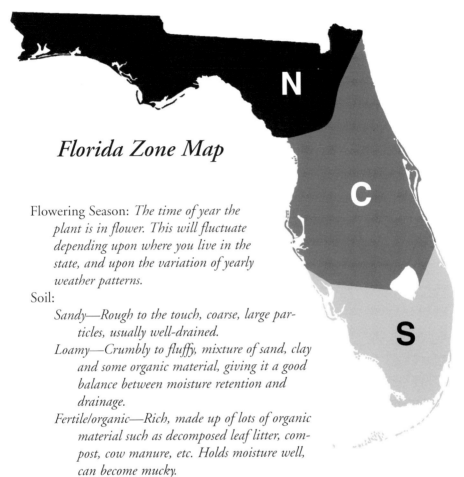

Florida Zone Map

Flowering Season: *The time of year the plant is in flower. This will fluctuate depending upon where you live in the state, and upon the variation of yearly weather patterns.*

Soil:

    Sandy—*Rough to the touch, coarse, large particles, usually well-drained.*

    Loamy—*Crumbly to fluffy, mixture of sand, clay and some organic material, giving it a good balance between moisture retention and drainage.*

    Fertile/organic—*Rich, made up of lots of organic material such as decomposed leaf litter, compost, cow manure, etc. Holds moisture well, can become mucky.*

Water: *Indicates the amount of water a plant needs to survive, once established.*

Establishment period: *The period of time between planting and new root growth. (See "Weekly Watering Guidelines" chart on page 16.)*

Light: *The range of lighting conditions under which the plant will grow.*

Salt Tolerance:

    High—*Can handle salt in the soil and occasional salt spray*

    Moderate—*Will tolerate small amounts of salt in soil, but needs protection from salt spray*

    Low—*Will suffer if exposed to salt spray or salt in the soil*

Propagation: *Easiest and most successful method of producing new plants.*

Plant With: *Just a small sampling of plants that will complement each other. Only those plants mentioned in this book are included. There are many others to choose from. Water, soil and light needs were taken into consideration in these recommendations.*

Weekly Watering Guidelines During the Establishment Period

WARM MONTHS: APRIL–OCTOBER				
	WEEK 1	WEEK 2–3	WEEK 4–6	WEEK 7–12
Ground covers, mass plantings	0.5" daily	0.5" every two days	0.75" twice a week	
Trees and shrubs in containers	fill basin twice per appl. daily	fill basin twice per appl. every two days	fill basin twice per appl. twice a week	
Trees and shrubs– ball & burlap	fill basin twice per appl. daily	fill basin twice per appl. every two days	fill basin twice per appl. every two days	fill basin twice per appl. twice a week

COOL MONTHS: NOVEMBER–MARCH				
	WEEK 1	WEEK 2–3	WEEK 4–6	WEEK 7–12
Ground covers, mass plantings	0.25" daily	0.5" twice a week	0.5" once a week	
Trees and shrubs in containers	fill basin once daily	fill basin once every 2 days	fill basin once, twice a week	
Trees and shrubs– ball & burlap	fill basin once daily	fill basin once every 2 days	fill basin once every 2 days	fill basin once, twice a week

Source: Southwest Florida Water Management District, "Water Requirements for Newly Planted Landscape Plants"

Butterflies and their Larval Plants

It is common for a male zebra butterfly to mate with a female while she is still inside her chrysalis. Here, two suitors attempt to mate with the same female.

Queen butterfly just after emerging. The veins that carry fluid from the abdomen into the wings are visible.

BRUSH-FOOTED BUTTERFLIES

Family Nymphalidae. This butterfly family includes a wide variety of butterflies, from the emerald-green malachite to the yellow-and-black zebra, as well as the monarch and queen butterflies. The one thing they all have in common is their tiny front legs, located close to head. Because this pair of legs is so small, brush-foots walk on four feet instead of six, like most other butterflies. The minute legs are sensitive to chemicals in certain plants, and help the females verify the identity of their larval food.

MILKWEED BUTTERFLIES

© BETTY WARGO

Monarch
Danaus plexippus
Family: Brush-footed butterfly
    (Nymphalidae)
Wingspan: 3.25" to 4.5"
Florida Range: Statewide
Season of Flight: Fall and spring
Preferred Habitat: Open fields
    and gardens
Adult Life Expectancy: 3 weeks
    to 6 months
Larval Foods: Milkweeds
    (*Asclepias* spp.), white vine
    (*Sarcostemma clausum*)

The monarch is without a doubt North America's most well-known butterfly species. Monarchs visit Florida during their spring and fall migrations, stopping to breed and feed along the way. You can welcome visiting monarchs (and the occasional stray or resident) to your garden with large plantings of milkweed. Monarch caterpillars are voracious; just a few of them can completely denude a four-foot tall milkweed plant in less than a day. Raising them is easy and fascinating. They increase to 3000 times their original size in a very short time. Monarchs and other adult

© AN ALLYN

butterflies also visit milkweed for the nectar its flowers produce. Another of the monarch's favorite nectar plants is goldenrod (*Solidago* spp.), which blooms during its fall migration.

Fire on the mountain! Imagine, flying high over the majestic Sierras near Michoacan, Mexico and witnessing the awesome sight of millions of orange monarchs falling toward the earth. That happened to businessman Ken Bruggers in 1973, yet it still took Bruggers, joined by biologist Fred Urquhart, two more years of intensive searching to find the winter home of monarchs migrating from eastern North America.

The migratory flight of the monarch has been studied for years, usually presenting more questions than answers. Do they navigate by the stars? Are they propelled forward by a magnetic field? Is it the sun that guides these tiny creatures the thousands of miles to their winter resting grounds? These are just a few of the theories that scientists have put forth in their quest to discover how the millions of monarch butterflies make their incredible journey year after year.

Research has found that the brood of butterflies that make the late summer/early fall migratory trip are definitely different from the earlier broods. These monarchs not only live much longer—some up to six months—they are also larger than their spring and summer counterparts. When they arrive in the Mexican mountains, the temperature is low and the butterflies relax into a semi-hibernation state, rarely consuming any food during their stay. Also, their sexual organs don't form until the following spring. They begin mating just after awakening from their winter slumber, before the return journey. Unfortunately this brood of fall butterflies will die en route, after depositing their eggs along the way. The butterflies from these eggs push farther north, yet it may take two or three generations to make it all the way back to the monarch's northernmost range in Canada. Then in the fall, the migratory cycle will begin again.

IDENTIFICATION: Adults have wings that are burnt orange with black veins on the upper and lower sides, with the upper wing surface distinctly brighter. White dots mark the black wing margins. Males are usually brighter in color than females. Caterpillars grow to be about two inches in length and have two pairs of black tubercles—fleshy, filamentlike projections—one pair protruding from the head and another from the tail. They have white, black and yellow stripes. The chrysalis is a beautiful emerald green with gold dots ringing the top. It becomes transparent when the butterfly is about to emerge. Eggs are pearly, oblong in shape, and have longitudinal ridges.

Queen ~ *Danaus gilippus*

Family: Brush-footed butterfly (Nymphalidae)
Wingspan: 3.0" to 4.5"
Florida Range: Statewide
Season of Flight: Spring through
fall in north and central
Florida; year round in south
Florida
Preferred Habitat: Open woods
and fields, sand dunes.
Adult Life Expectancy: 4 to 6 weeks
Larval Foods: Milkweeds
(*Asclepias* spp.), white vine
(*Sarcostemma clausum*)

© BETTY WARGO

Though not as well known as its
close relative the monarch, the
queen lives year round in Florida.
It does not like cold weather and
moves from north to south
Florida in late summer and early
fall. Though I have yet to see a
queen butterfly in my garden,
many of my friends have. I did once find a group of them at Fort DeSoto Park in
southern Pinellas County. The six butterflies were puddling so intently that I was
able to come within a few inches without disturbing them.

© JAN ALLYN

IDENTIFICATION: The upper and lower
sides of both fore- and hindwings are burnt
honey-brown . The underside is etched with
black veins. They are marked with white
spots along the edges and are rimmed with
black. The caterpillar has a distinct pattern
of black, yellow and white rings, and three
pairs of black tubercles. The chrysalis is similar to the monarch's, a striking green
marked with gold spots. The egg is pearly
white, oblong, with longitudinal ridges.

Milkweeds ~ *Asclepias* spp.

Family: Milkweed (Asclepiadaceae)
Plant Type: Herbaceous perennial
Florida Zones: N, C, S
Soil: Sandy, well-drained
Water: Drought tolerant after establish-
ment
Light: Full sun to partial shade
Mature Size (H x W): Varies with species
Salt Tolerance: Moderate
Flowering Season: Spring–fall (varies
with species)
Propagation: Seed

Although exotic scarlet milkweed (*Asclepias curassavica*) is often planted to attract monarchs, native Florida milkweeds are becoming easier to find in nurseries. Here are a few of them: Sandhill milkweed (*A. humistrata*) has clusters of white flowers and pale purple

A. humistrata

veins in its broad leaves. It requires well-drained soil and will die if it becomes too wet. Swamp milkweed (*A. incarnata*) is a tall milkweed with pink flowers that prefers rich, moist soil. Another popular milkweed that is also referred to as swamp milkweed is *A. perennis.* It will reach up to two feet tall, produces clusters of white flowers from spring through fall; it also grows well in rich, moist soil. My butterflyweed (*A. tuberosa*) is used more often as a nectar source by adult butterflies than as a larval food. It doesn't have the milky sap of other milkweeds, so perhaps it does not have enough toxin to protect caterpillars. Velvet-leaf milkweed

A. perennis

A. incarnata

(*A. tomentosa*) has hairy stems and leaves, and greenish flowers. It grows up to two feet high and also prefers sandy soil. Green-crowned milkweed (*A. viridis*) is an attractive, many-flowered plant. It has oblong leaves with wavy edges, and clusters of greenish-yellow flowers. It prefers rich, well-drained soil.

Most milkweeds grow best in full sun to lightly filtered shade. They are lovely planted with pentas, blazing star, goldenrod and ironweed. Milkweed may be grown from seed, with germination occurring quickly. Transplant seedlings when they are eight to ten inches tall. Group milkweed plants in large patches so caterpillars can move from plant to plant to forage for leaves. The survival rate of monarch caterpillars is very high, perhaps because of their toxicity. So even though milkweed plants seem able to replace their foliage quickly, it's important to have plenty available, expecially during the spring and fall migrations. I've received more than one frantic call from friends who have underestimated the appetites of these voracious creatures. No one likes to be stared down by ten hungry caterpillars gnawing on empty milkweed stalks. I've learned to keep pots of different milkweeds growing in various stages year-round to share with friends, and for a fast-food fill-in.

All species of milkweed are notoriously susceptible to aphid infestations. These tiny, yellow-orange, sucking insects damage the milkweed plants and may carry diseases that can be transferred to butterfly larvae. While chemical controls will kill the aphids, they also are also lethal to butterflies and caterpillars. Therefore, most butterfly gardeners opt to get rid of aphids with a carefully-directed blast from the garden hose, repeated at intervals as necessary. Another option is to use biological control, releasing ladybugs or green lacewing larvae. Both are well-known for their vast appetite for aphids.

Ladybug and aphids
on milkweed

PASSIONVINE BUTTERFLIES

© PHILIPPE OLIVIER

Gulf Fritillary ~ *Agraulis vanillae*

Family: Brush-footed butterfly (Nymphalidae)
Wingspan: 2.5" to 3.5"
Florida Range: Statewide
Season of Flight: All year
Preferred Habitat: Sunny gardens and open
    fields
Adult Life Expectancy: 1 to 3 weeks
Larval Foods: Passionvines (*Passiflora* spp.)

Gulf fritillaries are frequent visitors to gardens. These bursts of orange energy are well adapted to urban habitats. They are easy to attract and will stay year-round if you have plenty of passionvine, their host plant. They are also easy to raise. Look for caterpillars and yellow, oblong eggs on the tips of the long passionvine tendrils and on new growth. Gulf fritillaries prefer passionvine that's growing in a sunny spot, and have several broods during the year. Their flight is fast and erratic. They favor lantana, pentas and Spanish needle as nectar sources.

© JAN ALLYN

IDENTIFICATION:
Adult butterflies are orange. The upper sides of their wings have black spots, while the undersides have lovely silver markings and a sprinkling of black spots. The body of the gulf fritillary is a coppery orange with silvery white stripes. The orange caterpillars grow to a length of about two inches and have bluish- or brownish-black longitudinal stripes and black, branched, hairlike spines that are harmless but intimidating. Eggs are yellow, oblong and ribbed. The chrysalis is well disguised, resembling a crinkled, brown leaf.

Zebra
Heliconius charitonius
Family: Brush-footed butterfly
    (Nymphalidae)
Wingspan: 3.0" to 3.5"
Florida Range: Statewide
Season of Flight: All year
Preferred Habitat: Edge of
    woodlands, gardens, and
    tropical forests
Adult Life Expectancy: 1 to 6 months
Larval Foods: Passionvines (*Passiflora* spp.)

© BARBARA COLLINS

This black- and yellow-striped butterfly is a shade lover. It was named as Florida's official state butterfly in 1996. A "laid back," relaxed flyer, it is usually seen drifting slowly at the edges of shrubbery and trees. It is an easy species to photograph due to its leisurely nectaring pace and because zebras often rest or nectar with their wings spread wide. A year-round garden visitor, it is also one of the longest-lived Florida butterflies, with some individuals surviving six months. Unlike most other butterflies that just sip nectar, the zebra can also absorb the pollen that collects on its proboscis. This high-protein food helps it to produce eggs, and also may explain why it lives so long. Because the plant poisons they consumed as caterpillars make them nasty-tasting, most predators leave zebras alone. Their yellow, cone-shaped eggs are placed by females one at a time at the tips of new growth.

© DONALD TRAAS

IDENTIFICATION:
The caterpillar's coloration makes it hard to miss on the green leaves of passionvine. It is white, up to two inches long, marked with black dots and numerous black spines that warn off predators. The pupa stage of this butterfly is spent inside a chrysalis that looks like a dried up leaf with spines and two horns. The adult butterfly emerges five to ten days later. It is black with soft yellow stripes that run horizontally, with the bottom two rows being dotted. The underside of the hindwing has a pair of bright red spots at its base.

25

Julia ~ *Dryas iulia*

Family: Brush-footed butterfly
   (Nymphalidae)
Wingspan: 3.25" to 3.625"
Florida Range: South Florida
Season of Flight: All year
Preferred Habitat: Hammocks,
   fields, gardens
Adult Life Expectancy: 10 to 21 days
Larval Foods: Passionvines
   (*Passiflora* spp.)

Although julia butterflies are primarily south Florida residents, they may stray as far north as central Florida during summer months. They are common along the edges of hammocks and on islands, but also visit fields and residential gardens, where they may be attracted by nectar plants, especially those in shade or partial shade.

IDENTIFICATION: The julia butterfly has the gulf fritillary's orange color and the zebra's wide wingspan. Its wingtips are more pointed than those of the zebra, however, and the undersides of the julia's wings are a comparatively drab brown. Females are a duller orange than males. Each forewing has one, or sometimes two, black spots in the center, toward the leading edge of the wing. This spot (or spots) may be replaced by a black line on some females. The trailing

edge of the hindwings are narrowly edged in black. Caterpillars are a tan color, with fine black lines, black spots, and six rows of darker, branched spines. Eggs are pale yellow. The chrysalis is brown with flecks of gold, and looks like a dried-up leaf.

26

Passionvines ~ *Passiflora* spp.

Family: Passionflower (Passifloraceae)
Plant Type: Twining, perennial vine
Florida Zones: N, C, S
Soil: Sandy to organic, well-drained
Water: Drought tolerant once established
Light: Full sun to partial shade
Mature Size (H x W): Climbs to 15 feet
Salt Tolerance: High
Flowering Season: Spring through fall
Propagation: Seed or cuttings

P. incarnata

Maypop (*Passiflora incarnata*) is the star of Florida's native passionvines. Known for its extraordinary lavender and white flowers, it is a must for attracting any of the passionvine butterflies. It has three-lobed leaves and produces edible, egg-sized fruit. This sprawling vine dies back each winter and regrows every spring with—well, a passion. It will climb a trellis, cover a fence or ramble across a yard as a groundcover. It will also pop up in other places throughout your yard. I welcome the volunteers and pot them up to fill in bare spots or to share with friends.

P. suberosa

Yellow passionvine (*P. lutea*) occurs in north and central Florida. It isn't as flashy, but it is well loved by both zebras and the occasional julia stray, and is available year-round. Its tiny, greenish-yellow flowers are followed by deep purple fruit. I have many small pots of it around my deck, allowing me to easily watch and photograph zebras. This vine grows exceptionally well in the shade and is not fussy about soil type or moisture. In my yard I grow both these native passionvines, to provide plenty of enticement for female butterflies to visit and deposit their eggs. Corky-stemmed passionvine (*P. suberosa*) is common in central and south Florida and a favorite of the lovely julia, as well as zebra butterflies.

Red passionvine (*P. coccinea*) has very showy flowers but it is not native to Florida, it is not cold hardy, and as far as I know, it is not used as a larval food by caterpillars.

OTHER BRUSH-FOOTED BUTTERFLIES

© JAN ALLYN

Common Buckeye
Junonia coenia

Family: Brush-footed butterfly
(Nymphalidae)
Wingspan: 2.0" to 2.5"
Florida Range: Statewide
Season of Flight: All year, but
more prevalent in summer
Preferred Habitat: Pine woods,
open fields and gardens
Adult Life Expectancy: 5 days to
3 weeks
Larval Foods: Twinflower
(*Dychoriste oblongifolia*), wild petunia (*Ruellia caroliniensis*), blue toadflax
(*Linaria canadensis*), southern plantain (*Plantago virginica*), false foxglove
(*Agalinis* spp.), snapdragon (*Antirrhinum majus*)

Although the colorful buckeye butterfly is relatively small, it is adorned with large, bold eyespots. These help protect it by confusing its predators. The buckeye likes to bask in the sun and is often seen with its wings spread open, resting on a flower, rock or even a warm driveway. Truly a "social butterfly," it isn't put off by competition. I observed a buckeye and a zebra swallowtail nectaring side-by-side from the same flower. Look for buckeyes on these favorite nectar sources: buddleia (*Buddleia* spp.), redroot (*Lachnanthes caroliniana*), and Spanish needle (*Bidens pilosa*). One of the buckeye's springtime larval foods is blue toadflax (*Linaria canadensis*). This common wildflower is in the same family as the snapdragon (Scrophulariaceae). It appears in bunches along roadsides, open fields and front yards in late winter and spring. The tiny flowers are light blue, brushed with white.

© ROBIN COLE/COLEPHOTO

Linaria canadensis

While the buckeye occurs throughout most of the United States, two of its close relatives are more tropical. Both are very similar in appearance to the buckeye, but have much smaller eyespots. The mangrove buckeye (*J. evarete*) is found in coastal mangrove forests of central and south Florida. Black mangrove

(*Avicennia germanis*) is its larval food. The eyespots on its forewings are completely encircled by orange. The tropical buckeye (*J. genoveva*) is found only in extreme south Florida and the Keys. Its larval foods include porterweed (*Stachytarpheta jamaicensis*), wild petunia (*Ruellia caroliniensis*) and capeweed (*Lippia* spp.).

© DONALD TRAAS

IDENTIFICATION: The buckeye is dusky brown above and below. Pairs of bright, orange-red, epaulet-like bars adorn the upper surface of the forewings; each bar is outlined in black. Each forewing also has a pale, irregular band with a dark eye-spot. Each fore- and hindwing has one large and one smaller eyespot, the largest of these, on the hindwings, being bold and multi-colored—orange, pink and lavender, ringed by a pale band and a black one. Buckeye caterpillars are brown-black with orange markings and fuzzy black hairs. When they feed on the long, wispy stalks of false foxglove, they are well camouflaged. It's not unusual to see five caterpillars of various sizes feeding on the same stem. Buckeye eggs are green, and the chrysalis is light brown.

© JAN ALLYN

Twinflower
Dyschoriste oblongifolia
Family: Acanthus (Acanthaceae)
Plant Type: Herbaceous perennial
Florida Zones: N, C, S
Mature Size (H): 8 inches
Flowering Season: Spring through fall
Soil: Sandy, well-drained
Water: Drought tolerant once established
Light: Full sun to partial shade
Salt Tolerance: Low
Propagation: Seed, division

Twinflower is a very low-growing groundcover with soft green leaves and small, five-lobed flowers of a delicate lavender color dotted with purple. It reseeds readily and will spread to cover an area. Twinflower's blossoms usually open in pairs, giving it its common name. It is virtually carefree, thriving without fertilizer and with very little water. Although it does not completely die back in winter, it does become dormant, the leaves taking on a rusty color and the plants generally becoming less vigorous.

© ROBIN COLE/COLEPHOTO

Malachite
Siproeta stelenes

Family: Brush-footed butterfly
(Nymphalidae)
Wingspan: 2.5" to 4.0"
Florida Range: Extreme south
Florida and the Florida Keys
Season of Flight: All year
Preferred Habitat: Tropical
hammocks, gardens, wood-
land edges
Adult Life Expectancy: 4 days
to 2 weeks
Larval Foods: Wild petunia
(*Ruellia caroliniensis*),
Blechum *(Blechum
pyramidatum)*

A jewel on the wing, this butterfly is named after the green mineral malachite. When freshly emerged from its chrysalis, the malachite is startlingly brilliant in color, but its brightness pales as it ages. The sight of it conjures images of lush rain forests—it's hard to forget. Though usually found skimming woodland edges and in citrus groves, the malachite may be lured to the garden by a large display of colorful nectar plants. Some researchers believe resident malachite populations in south Florida and the Keys originated from strays from Cuba or Mexico.

IDENTIFICATION: The upper sides of the wings are translucent green and are out-lined with deep, chocolate brown. Females are lighter in color than males. The undersides of the wings are almost as vibrant, light brown marked with pale green and creamy white. The malachite caterpillar is black with red spines and has two red horns on its head. Eggs are green, and the chrysalis is bright green.

© DALE McCLUNG

© DALE McCLUNG

Wild Petunia ~ *Ruellia caroliniensis*

Family: Acanthus (Acanthaceae)
Plant Type: Herbaceous perennial
Florida Zones: N, C, S
Soil: All soil types
Water: Drought tolerant after estab-
    lishment
Light: Full sun to partial shade
Mature Size (H x W): 1 ft. x 1 ft.
Salt Tolerance: High
Flowering Season: All year in south
    Florida, spring through fall in
    north Florida
Propagation: Seed, or cuttings taken
    in summer

Wild petunia takes its name from its
lavender flowers, which resemble
cultivated petunias, but are smaller.
This marvelous plant thrives on gentle neglect, blooming under widely
varying conditions—sun or shade,
wet or dry, sandy or organic soil.
The delicate, short-lived flowers usu-
ally open early in the day, then fall off before nightfall. Plant several wild petunias in a group so you will always have some flowers. Wild petunia is very easy to
cultivate, readily reseeds, and will fill an area nicely by the second season.
Though it will grow in almost any soil, it will grow larger and produce more
flowers in richer soil. Individual plants vary considerably in form, some being
compact and bushy while others are more rangy.

Red Admiral ~ *Vanessa atalanta*

Family: Brush-footed butterfly
  (Nymphalidae)
Wingspan: 1.5" to 2.25"
Florida Range: Statewide
Season of Flight: All year
Preferred Habitat: Open, moist areas, marsh-
  es, streams
Adult Life Expectancy: 1 to 3 weeks
Larval Foods: Nettles (*Urtica* spp.), false net-
  tles (*Boehmeria* spp.), pellitories
  (*Parietaria* spp.)

Although red admirals are relatively small butterflies, they are strong, acrobatic flyers. Very territorial, they fly at anything that strays into their "space." Individual butterflies are often seen basking on rocks. Last summer a red admiral adopted the west rim of my above-ground swimming pool as its basking spot. Every afternoon for a week, it would return to its chosen observation point and survey the area. Then, as suddenly as it appeared, my solitary visitor was gone. Red admirals are notorious for alighting on people. At a local garden center I saw a red admiral boldly land on a woman's shoulder as she selected plants. Looking like a colorful brooch, the butterfly rode along, its host completely unaware of it. The red admiral's larval food plant is the nettle. The true nettle is an undesirable plant in the garden because of its stinging spines, but you may choose to grow false nettle for caterpillars, if you have a boggy site in which to plant it. You can also attract red admirals by planting lots of butterfly bush (*Buddleia* spp.), one of its favorite nectar sources.

IDENTIFICATION: Wings are a dusky brown-black above, brightened by a band of orange that slashes across each forewing, and by splashes of white near each wingtip. Each hindwing also has a conspicuous band of orange that runs along the rear edge, punctuated by small black dots. Both fore- and hindwing margins are scalloped, rimmed in white. The underside of the red admiral is completely different, a swirled mixture of black, brown and white. The forewing is marked by three colored patches, one pink, one blue and one white. Caterpillars have black and white spines. Their coloration varies considerably among individuals and may include black, yellow, gray, green or white. They use leaves of their host plant to build nests of silk for protection, replacing each shelter as it is outgrown. Red admiral eggs are green, and the chrysalis is brown with gold spots.

© ROBIN COLE/COLEPHOTO

False Nettle
Boehmeria cylindrica
Family: Nettle (Urticaceae)
Plant Type: Herbaceous perennial
Florida Zones: N, C, S
Mature Size (H): 3 feet
Flowering Season: Spring through fall
Soil: Fertile, loamy
Water: Requires moist site or frequent
    irrigation
Light: Partial shade
Salt Tolerance: Unknown
Propagation: Seeds, root division

False nettle is not a particularly attractive landscape plant and is unlikely to be found in any nursery. Its spikes of greenish flowers are rather nondescript and it has a weedy appearance. However, those who have a pond or other wet area on or abutting their property and want to attract red admirals may want to plant false nettle or encourage wild plants to grow there. Members of your local Florida Native Plant Society chapter who are butterfly gardeners may be able to help you locate specimens.

White Peacock
Anartia jatrophae
Family: Brush-footed butterfly
(Nymphalidae)
Wingspan: 2" to 3"
Florida Range: Peninsular Florida
Season of Flight: All year, except in cold
weather
Preferred Habitat: Banks of ponds and streams, open fields
Adult Life Expectancy: 10 days to 2 weeks
Larval Foods: Water hyssop (*Bacopa* spp.), wild petunia (*Ruellia caroliniensis*).

I have come so close to a pair of these little butterflies that it was hard not to
reach right out and touch them. The best places to look for white peacock butterflies is around lakes, ponds, streams, bays or bogs because their favorite larval

food, water hyssop, grows there. The white peacock's lazy flight is usually close to the ground.
For that reason they tend to visit small shrubs and
low-growing plants. On my daily walks along
Old Tampa Bay, I used to see plenty of these butterflies among low-growing nectar flowers such as
frog fruit. In the last few years, however, man-
grove-trimming, disallowed for many years, was
approved. In their desire to have an open view of
the bay, many well-intentioned homeowners not
only trimmed their mangroves, but ripped out all the transitory vegetation around
them, replacing it with high-maintenance lawn. Unfortunately, this destroyed
much of the white peacock butterfly's nectar and larval food. The local population has suffered greatly and now I'm lucky to spot one or two butterflies a day.

IDENTIFICATION: Its elaborate wing markings give the white peacock its name.
The upper and lower surfaces of both fore- and hindwings are white, dusted and
streaked with brown, with orange and brown bands along the wing edges. Small,
dark brownish-black eyespots are rimmed in pale orange. Adults are seen all year
in south Florida and during warmer months elsewhere. Caterpillars are black
with silvery-white markings and spines. Eggs of the white peacock are light yellow, and the chrysalis is smooth and dark green.

© JAN ALLYN

Water hyssop ~ *Bacopa* spp.

Family: Snapdragon (Scrophulariaceae)
Plant Type: Aquatic perennial herb
Florida Zones: N, C, S
Soil: Organic
Water: Wet
Light: Full sun to partial shade
Mature Size (H): 4 in. (will form a mat)
Salt Tolerance: High
Flowering Season: All year
Propagation: By cuttings, taken after
    plant has established roots.

There are several species of water hyssop that you can grow. They are best placed in a bog garden or around a pond, as this plant's natural habitat is in very wet areas. One species of water hyssop (*B. monnieri*) has white flowers that are brushed with pink and have yellow centers. Its stems and leaves are fleshy and succulent. Another, lemon bacopa (*B. caroliniana*) has tiny, vase-like, sky-blue flowers. As its name implies, the leaves smell lemony when crushed. Because of its flowers, it is also called blue hyssop.

Hyssops are great for those that have a pond, small bog or other water feature on their property. If you don't, you can grow water hyssop in a container. I have some in a pot that sits in a water-filled pan, thus keeping the soil moist at all times. These plants are very easy to propagate. Simply break a piece off and stick it in wet soil.

American Lady
Vanessa virginiensis

Family: Brush-footed butterfly
  (Nymphalidae)
Wingspan: 1.75" to 2.25"
Florida Range: Statewide
Season of Flight: Late spring to fall
Preferred Habitat: Gardens and
  open fields
Adult Life Expectancy: 1 to 3 weeks
Larval Foods: Uses a number of dif-
  ferent plants, among them
  smooth-leaved asters (family
  Asteraceae), cudweed
  (*Gnaphalium* spp.) and some
  members of the mallow family
  (Malvaceae).

The best way to attract American lady butterflies to your garden is to plant large masses of the same nectar plant. These butterflies are very active and move constantly while nectaring, making them tough to photograph but comical to watch. They "march" around a

flower like tiny drill sargeants, wings held upright, never completely at rest. They are very protective about their space and will fly right at intruders, be they large or small. American lady caterpillars have their own interesting habit. They build nests to protect themselves, using the leaves of their larval food as material. The nests expand as the larva grows, and the chrysalis sometimes forms inside the nest.

IDENTIFICATION: The American lady is a small butterfly. The upper surfaces of its wings are orange, tinged slightly with pink, with intricate black-brown markings along the edges. White spots and small dashes mark the forewings. On the underside of the wings are large blue eyespots and a bold pink patch on a background that is a swirl of soft white and muted brown. American lady caterpillars are black, marked with yellowish-green bands and spots that are white and reddish-brown. It has black, branched spines that deter predators but are harmless. Eggs are greenish yellow, and the chrysalis is brown, flecked with gold.

© ROBIN COLE/COLEPHOTO

Cudweed ~ *Gnaphalium* spp.
Family: Aster (Asteraceae)
Plant Type: Annual wildflower
Florida Zones: N, C, S
Soil: Sandy, well-drained
Water: Drought tolerant
Light: Full sun
Salt Tolerance: Moderate
Mature Size: 1 ft. x 1 ft.
Flowering Season: Summer, Fall
Propagation: Seed

Cudweed is an annual wildflower that has fuzzy, silvery-green leaves and nondescript white or brownish flower bracts. Although it's a common weed, I never would have noticed it if not for my interest in butterflies. Examine your yard, it may already be growing there. It propagates readily from seed and will form clumps if given enough room. Two species (*G. pensylvanicum* and *G. falcatum*) are very similar, with grayish stems and hairy leaves. Sweet everlasting (*G. obtusifolium*), also known as rabbit tobacco, is a bit taller and has narrower leaves. Look for plants on roadsides and disturbed areas and collect the seed, remembering to get permission from the landowner and to leave at least three-quarters of the seed on each plant. Members of your local native plant society also may have seed to share. Sow it directly in your garden in the fall. Although cudweed isn't especially showy, it will be appreciated by the American ladies that visit your garden. No fertilizer is needed and will harm this plant if applied. Don't pamper cudweed and you'll have success with it.

Florida Viceroy
Limenitis archippus floridensis

Family: Brush-footed butterfly (Nymphalidae)
Wingspan: 3" to 3.5"
Florida Range: Statewide
Season of Flight: All year
Preferred Habitat: Marshes, streams, swampy areas
Adult Life Expectancy: 10 days to 2 weeks
Larval Foods: Coastal plain willow (*Salix caroliniana*), black willow (*Salix nigra*)

© BETTY WARGO

If you happen to live near a stream, canal or marshy area where willow grows, chances are you've seen lots of viceroy butterflies already. The viceroy practices a type of mimicry called Mullerian, named after Fritz Muller who discovered that certain species that all tasted repugnant to predators also had very similar coloration and markings. Once a predator attempted to eat any of the species, it forever remembered its mistake and left all similar species alone, even those that were not unpalatable. The Florida viceroy looks very much like the well-known monarch butterfly, but in areas where the queen butterfly population is larger, it will mimic the darker brown coloration of the queen.

IDENTIFICATION: This butterfly looks almost the same on top as it does on the bottom. Its wings are a deep reddish-brown, lined with thick black vines. The tips have a wide edging of black, sprinkled with white dots. Underneath, the white marks look more like tiny boomerangs. Even though Florida viceroys are occasionally mistaken for monarchs, the black semicircular bands that cut across their wings easily distinguish them. The caterpillars are grayish-brown and white, resembling bird droppings. They have two small, hairy, black horns and numerous bumps on their backs. Even as a chrysalis the Florida viceroy retains its bird-dropping camouflage. It is mottled brown, marked with what looks like a white saddle.

© ROBIN COLE/COLEPHOTO

38

© JAN ALYN

Coastal Plain Willow ~ *Salix caroliniana*

Plant Type: Deciduous tree
Florida Zones: N, C, S
Mature Size (H x W): 20 ft. x 20 ft.
Flowering Season: Spring
Soil: Organic
Water: Moist
Light: Full sun
Salt Tolerance: High
Propagation: Cuttings, seed

This small tree is often found at the edges of streams, rivers, lakes and ponds. It prefers this damp, swampy locale and will tolerate occasional flooding. An area that receives plenty of moisture yet is fairly well-drained will work best. Like other willows, the branches of the coastal plain willow tend to bend toward the ground. The leaf gall to which this tree is susceptible helps to camouflage the viceroy's eggs. The male blossoms, or catkins, are greenish-yellow and showy, but short-lived. Sawgrass Lake Park in central Pinellas County is one of those magical butterfly spots. Its wooden boardwalk gently winds through a willow tree forest. The tangled limbs frequently spill over the railings, providing a butterfly enthusiast ample opportunity to find viceroy caterpillars. I have yet to visit without seeing both the adult viceroy and its larvae.

SWALLOWTAIL BUTTERFLIES

Family Papilionidae. Large and beautiful, the swallowtail butterflies' long, sweeping tails are reminiscent of the swallow, the bird they are named after. Out of the hundreds of swallowtail species worldwide, about ten are seen in Florida. This includes the endangered Schaus' swallowtail, found only in the extreme southern tip of the Florida peninsula and in the Keys. All the swallowtail butterflies in the state of Florida have long tails except the polydamas (gold rim). Another characteristic common to swallowtails is the presence of fleshy, spike-like osmeteria used by their caterpillars to deter predators. These two "horns," located behind the caterpillar's head, pop out and emit a nasty odor when the caterpillar is disturbed. Swallowtail pupae hang upright, attached to a twig or leaf with a strand of silk.

©JOHN & GLORIA TVETEN/KAC PRODUCTIONS

Palamedes Swallowtail ~ *Pterourus palamedes*
(Papilionidae)

...wide, except keys and prairie areas
Season of flight: All year
Preferred Habitat: Wet woodlands, swampy areas
Adult Life Expectancy: 5 days to 2 weeks
Larval Foods: Spicebush (*Lindera* spp.), red bay (*Persea borbonia*), swamp bay
 (*Persea palustris*), silk bay (*Persea borbonia* var. *humilis*)

This is a fairly common swallowtail butterfly that will visit your garden often, especially if your property abuts a marshy area. Plant some red bay, swamp bay or spicebush alongside water-loving nectar plants to lure the lovely palamedes butterfly. If you live in a dry, scrubby area, plant silk bay. I saw a silk bay specimen at Environmental Equities, a plant nursery in Hudson, that was loaded with catepillars hiding in the folded leaves. The palamedes is another butterfly that uses mimicry as a defense against predators. The markings on the underside of its wings resemble those of the foul-tasting pipevine swallowtail.

IDENTIFICATION: Upper sides are dusky black. Forewings are rounded and have a double row of yellow spots along the edge. A prominent yellow band on the hindwings ends in a small blue eyespot. The abdomen has black and yellow stripes. Caterpillars at first resemble bird droppings, but after several instars become brilliant green with black eyespots meant to discourage predators. The palamedes caterpillar protects itself by folding a leaf over and hiding inside, as does the caterpillar of the spicebush swallowtail. Eggs are greenish yellow, and the chrysalis is greenish-gray.

Spicebush Swallowtail ~ *Pterourus troilus*

Family: Swallowtail (Papilionidae)
Wingspan: 3.5" to 4.5"
Florida Range: All of Florida, except Miami area to the Keys
Season of Flight: March through December
Preferred Habitat: Woodlands, gardens, meadows
Adult Life Expectancy: 1 to 2 weeks
Larval Foods: Spicebush (*Lindera* spp.), sassafras (*Sassafras albidum*), possibly red bay (*Persea borbonia*), swamp bay (*Persea palustris*)

Adult spicebush swallowtails are often found near wet woodlands where their larval food is plentiful. If your property is close to a pond, creek or other wet area, consider planting buttonbush there as a butterfly nectar source. Spicebush swallowtails and many other species of butterflies will be attracted by the round, white, fragrant blossoms of this water-loving, native shrub. Spicebush swallowtails mimic the appearance of the bad-tasting pipevine swallowtail, a ruse that protects them from predators.

Spicebush swallowtail caterpillars are my favorites. Although they begin life looking like bird droppings, by their last instar they have been completely transformed. The change begins when the caterpillars are about an inch long. They turn a brilliant green and spots appear just behind the head. These eventually resemble the eyes of a snake, markings designed to frighten off predators. As an additional deterrent, forked red horns called osmeteria pop out from the top of the caterpillar's head if it is threatened, and a nasty odor blankets the unsuspecting intruder.

IDENTIFICATION: Adults are black, marked with creamy light-yellow spots on the outer edges of the upper front and hind wings. An orange eye-spot is located at the bottom inner edge of the hind wings. Although both males and females are marked with sparkling, blue-green scales on their upper hind wings, they are somewhat bluer on the female. The tails of both sexes are black. Two rows of orange-red spots mark the underside of the wings, reminiscent of the single row of spots present on the toxic pipevine swallowtail. Spicebush swallowtail eggs are light green, and the chrysalis is green or brown.

Sassafras ~ *Sassafras albidum*

Family: Laurel (Lauraceae)
Plant Type: Shrub or small tree
Florida Zones: N, C
Soil: Acid, well-drained, sandy to
    organic
Water: Drought tolerant after
    establishment
Light: Full sun to partial shade
Mature Size (H x W): 15 ft. x 10 ft.
Salt Tolerance: Low
Flowering Season: Spring
Propagation: Root cuttings

Scratch the bark of sassafras and you'll inhale the scent of a tall glass of icy-cold root beer. In northern climates this tree may reach 60 feet in height, but in Florida and other southern states it rarely exceeds 15 feet and usually takes a shrubby form. Sassafras is an understory plant that thrives in mature, open, hardwood forests. It is more common in north Florida but will grow as far south as Tampa. Since sassafras spreads by underground roots, plant several together to create a nice thicket in the corner of your garden. To keep them manageable, simply use a mower to trim unwanted sprouts. The yellow-orange and red leaves provide a wonderful show in the fall. The ground roots of sassafras are used to make filé, the spice that flavors and thickens an authentic gumbo.

Spicebush ~ *Lindera benzoin*

Family: Laurel (Lauraceae)
Plant Type: Deciduous shrub
Florida Zones: N
Soil: Fertile, slightly alkaline
Water: Requires regular
    irrigation
Light: Full or partial shade
Mature Size (H x W):
    8 ft. x 8 ft.
Salt Tolerance: Unknown
Flowering Season: Spring
Propagation: Seeds, cuttings

Spicebush provides landscape color in the form of springtime yellow flowers, golden yellow fall foliage, and bright red berries. It gets its common name from the spicy aroma of its leaves, which are grayish-green below and are often covered with tiny hairs. Spicebush is dioecious, meaning that both male and female plants are needed for pollination. Yellow flowers are borne in dense clusters in early spring and are especially striking because they appear before the new leaf growth emerges. The female plants bear the fruit and are therefore more attractive. Spicebush berries are oblong, about a quarter-inch in length. They ripen by early fall and are very attractive to birds. Spicebush is a perfect specimen shrub for a shady, woodsy, naturalized setting.

Red bay ~ *Persea borbonia*

Family: Laurel (Lauraceae)
Plant Type: Large, evergreen tree
Florida Zones: N, C, S
Mature Size (H x W): 40 ft. x 40 ft.
Flowering Season: Spring
Soil: Acid, sandy
Water: Water well to establish, then as needed
Light: Full sun to partial shade
Salt Tolerance: High
Propagation: Seed

Red bay is a lovely shade tree with shiny, deep green leaves. They are fragrant and may be used in cooking or potpourri. If you choose to plant this tree near your butterfly garden, place it far enough away that it won't shade your nectar plants. I planted a red bay sapling near the butterfly garden at my daughter's elementary school. Although narrow, the tree was almost six feet tall by its second year. Leaf gall sometimes affects red bays, but it's usually not a serious problem. Red bay is tolerant of both drought and periodic flooding, and is not fussy about soil composition. If you have a really wet area, use swamp bay (*Persea palustris*), a water-loving tree that may grow to 30 feet or more. If your property has the opposite conditions, very dry, well-drained, sandy soil, plant silk bay (*Persea borbonia* var. *humilis*). Silk bay will grow to about 30 feet; its shiny leaves have brown, fuzzy hairs on the undersides.

© RICHARD DAY/DAYBREAK IMAGERY

Black Swallowtail
Papilio polyxenes
Family: Swallowtail
   (Papilionidae)
Wingspan: 2.5" to 5.0"
Florida Range: Statewide
Season of Flight: All year
Preferred Habitat: Wet
   fields, gardens, meadows
   and marshy areas
Adult Life Expectancy:
   5 days to 2 weeks
Larval Foods: Parsley, dill,
   fennel

Black swallowtails are often attracted to herb gardens, as they lay their eggs on members of the carrot family like parsley, fennel and dill. If you don't mind sharing your herbs, choose to welcome their arrival. The pudgy caterpillars are often the target of predators, unprotected as they are by plant toxins. Eluding predators continues through adulthood. Because they are so large, black swallowtail butterflies present quite a meal opportunity to hungry birds. It's not unusual to see swallowtails with tattered wings, damage sometimes caused by a predator's near-miss. Lured by the brilliant eyespots at the base of the wings, a bird usually ends up with a mouthful of wing instead of a juicy meal.

IDENTIFICATION: The upper surface of the wings of the black swallowtail is deep blue-black. The male has a prominent yellow band stretching almost from wingtip to wingtip. This band is either very light or absent on females. Both sexes have a dusting of iridescent blue near the edge of the hindwing, the female being somewhat brighter. Two noticeable orange eyespots dot the base of the wings, just below the body. The underside of the wings is black, with orange and pale yellow spots and a dusting of blue. The wing margins are edged in white. The body is black with a row of pale yellow spots along each side of the abdomen. Coloration of the female black swallowtail resembles that of the pipevine swallowtail. This mimicry helps to protect it from predators who shy away from the bad-tasting pipevine swallowtail. Caterpillars start out black with orange spots, and

© JAN ALLYN

have one white band in the middle that resembles a saddle. However, they don't remain that color for long, changing with each instar and finally becoming yellow, black, white and green striped. Like many other swallowtails, they have osmeteria, a pair of scent glands behind the head that protrude and emit a foul odor if the caterpillar feels threatened. Black swallowtail eggs are creamy-white to yellow. The chrysalis is gray-brown or drab green, and looks like a curled leaf.

Parsley, dill, fennel

Family: Carrot (Apiaceae)
Plant Type: Varies
Florida Zones: N, C, S
Soil: Organic
Water: Keep moist but not wet
Light: Full sun
Salt Tolerance: None
Mature Size (H x W): 1 ft. x 1 ft. (parsley),
    5 ft. x 3 ft. (dill and fennel)
Flowering Season: Varies
Propagation: Seed

Wild plants from the carrot family are hard to find at nurseries, but you can plant the culinary herbs above to satisfy the hunger pangs of black swallowtail larvae. I have had great success attracting butterflies to my parsley, dill and fennel plants. Dill and fennel have very attractive, wispy foliage. They grow up to five feet tall and may require staking. I grow dill and fennel in the ground, and keep parsley in pots. I have found that pots of parsley placed up off the ground (about three feet high) seemed to have more eggs laid on them than parsley planted at ground level. Mix garden soil with dehydrated cow manure in a one-to-one ratio for parsley and other potted plants that like organic soil. Herbs are a cool weather crop in most of Florida. Some herb gardeners give up in summer, but I like to keep my black swallowtails supplied with food, even in hot weather. I protect my herbs from the summer's heat by moving them to a cooler, shadier part of my yard.

© JAN ALLYN

Eastern Tiger Swallowtail ~ *Pterourus glaucus*

Family: Swallowtail (Papilionidae)
Wingspan: 3.5" to 5.5"
Florida Range: All of Florida, except for Florida Keys
Season of Flight: Spring through fall
Preferred Habitat: Swamps, gardens and woodland edges
Adult Life Expectancy: 1 to 2 weeks
Larval Foods: Black cherry (*Prunus serotina*), sweet bay (*Magnolia virginiana*),
    tulip tree (*Liriodendron tulipifera*)

Although common, eastern tiger swallowtails are very beautiful. They are easily
recognizable, even in flight, because of the prominent black and yellow markings
on their wings. High fliers, they are found throughout the eastern United States
as far north as the Great Lakes. In Florida they are less prevalent on the east coast
than elsewhere. Often seen in fields of wildflowers, they are are easily enticed to
visit butterfly gardens. Adults will feed from a variety of nectar flowers. In my
own garden, I find that they are particularly attracted to ironweed.

IDENTIFICATION: This butterfly is named for the four black, vertical slashes that
cut across its powdery yellow wings. The outer edges of the wings are broadly
banded in black, with yellow spots in the margins. The abdomen has vertical
black and yellow stripes. Some females have dark coloration, with mimicry play-
ing a role. These females are mostly black, with a dusting of blue on the hindwings and the rear portion of the forewings. This pattern closely resembles the
markings of the pipevine swallowtail, and it is thought that the mimicry occurs
in areas heavily populated by these distasteful butterflies. Caterpillars look like
bird droppings at first, but when mature are light green and blend in well with
their larval food. Two small eyespots on the head help deter predators. Eggs are
greenish-yellow and globular in shape. The chrysalis may be green or brown.

Black Cherry ~ *Prunus serotina*
Family: Rose (Rosaceae)
Plant Type: Large tree
Florida Zones: N, C
Soil: Organic, well drained
Water: Moist site or regular irrigation
Light: Full sun to partial shade
Mature Size (H x W): 50 ft. x 15 ft.
Salt Tolerance: Moderate
Flowering Season: Spring
Propagation: Tip cuttings, seed

This wild cherry is a beautiful tree that can grow to 100 feet, though it rarely attains that height in Florida. Its leaves turn a vibrant orange-red in the fall. Fragrant, white bottle-brush-like blossoms appear in spring. They provide nectar for butterflies but are very short-lived. The purple fruit is a treat for birds and other wildlife—however, the rest of the plant is poisonous. Black cherry tolerates some shade and doesn't mind being crowded. The trees in my own yard are located between large oaks and have managed to grow almost straight up toward the sun.

Sweet Bay ~ *Magnolia virginiana*
Family: Magnolia (Magnoliaceae)
Plant Type: Large evergreen tree
Florida Zones: N, C, S
Soil: Moist, fertile
Water: Moist site or regular irrigation
Light: Full sun to partial shade
Mature Size (H x W): 50 ft. x 15 ft.
Salt Tolerance: Low
Flowering Season: Summer
Propagation: Seed

© JAN ALLYN

In addition to providing food for eastern tiger swallowtail larvae, sweet bay has other fine qualities. It has creamy white, showy, fragrant flowers nearly three inches across, and aromatic leaves that can be used in cooking. Its evergreen foliage is attractive, with large leaves that are shiny and deep green above and a silvery color below. Sweet bay does have some drawbacks; it is not tolerant of drought, it tends to produce suckers, and its narrow crown does not produce much shade.

Tulip Tree ~ *Liriodendron tulipifera*

Family: Magnolia (Magnoliaceae)
Plant Type: Large, flowering, deciduous tree
Florida Zones: N, C
Mature Size (H x W): 75 ft. x 25 ft.
Flowering Season: Spring
Soil: Loamy, rich
Water: Moist site or regular
    irrigation
Light: Full sun
Salt Tolerance: Low
Propagation: Seed, cuttings

Other common names for
this tree are tulip poplar and
yellow poplar, but the tulip
tree is not a poplar at all,
nor is it closely related to
them; they are members of
the willow family (Salicaceae). Although they require fertile, loamy, moist soil,
tulip trees are intolerant of flooding. Their large flowers are an unusual combination of green and orange, and the leaves are also quite characteristic, each having
four or six squarish lobes. The conspicuous flowers and bright green leaves offer a
colorful springtime show. Tulip trees in more temperate climates may attain
tremendous heights—over 200 feet. Florida specimens are typically much smaller, even though they are relatively fast growing. They are not well suited for south
Florida and occur only sporadically in central Florida, although if well situated
and cared for they may be grown as far south as Orlando.

ॐ✿ॐ

Giant Swallowtail ~ *Heraclides cresphontes*

Family: Swallowtail (Papilionidae)
Wingspan: 4.0" to 5.5"
Florida Range: Statewide
Season of Flight: All year, though less common in winter
Preferred Habitat: Woodlands, gardens, citrus groves
Adult Life Expectancy: 5 days to 2 weeks
Larval Foods: Citrus cultivars (*Citrus* spp.), Hercules' club (*Zanthoxylum clava-herculis*), wild lime (*Zanthoxylum fagara*), torchwood (*Amyris elemifera*)

© JAN ALLYN

The giant swallowtail is among the largest butterflies in North America, dwarfing most of the flowers on which it nectars. It does a delicate balancing act, clinging precariously to a blossom while constantly beating its wings to stay aloft. Though giant swallowtails may visit low-growing flowers or shrubs to nectar, they prefer treetops when it comes to laying their eggs. Their frequent appearance in citrus groves has earned them the nickname "orange dog." The larvae feed on both native and cultivated members of the citrus family.

IDENTIFICATION: Upper sides of the wings are dark brown-black, with prominent yellow bands. One runs horizontally across the forewings from wingtip to wingtip. Each hindwing is also banded with yellow. Giant swallowtails are easily recognized by their powdery-yellow undersides. The underwings are marked with black bands, and each "tail" has a yellow eyespot. The beautiful adults are a far cry from the caterpillars, which are rather ugly and look like bird droppings, a clever camouflage. The caterpillars also have orange-red osmeteria to help protect them from predation. Eggs are pale yellow-green. The chrysalis is grayish-brown and resembles a small piece of twig.

© ROBIN COLE/COLEPHOTO

50

Wild Lime ~ *Zanthoxylum fagara*

Family: Citrus (Rutaceae)
Plant Type: Small evergreen tree
Florida Zones: C, S
Mature Size: 25 ft. x 15 ft.
Flowering Season: All year
Soil: Sandy to slightly organic
Water: Drought tolerant once
    established
Light: Full sun
Salt Tolerance: High
Propagation: Seeds, root cuttings

© JAN ALLYN

The leaves of wild lime have a pleasant lime odor when crushed, however it does not produce an edible fruit. Like its close relative Hercules' club, it is very thorny. It is not especially frost tolerant but can be grown in central Florida in protected areas. It has rounded, compound leaves and small, greenish-yellow flowers that produce nectar for butterflies and pollen for bees and other insects. Birds relish the shiny black seeds, which ripen by fall. Like some kinds of cultivated citrus, wild lime has winglike appendages at the base of each leaf stem.

© ROBIN COLE/COLEPHOTO

Hercules' Club
Zanthoxylum clava-herculis

Family: Citrus (Rutaceae)
Plant Type: Small deciduous tree
Florida Zones: N, C, S
Mature Size (H x W): 20 ft. x 15 ft.
Flowering Season: Spring
Soil: Sandy to slightly organic
Water: Drought tolerant after establishment
Light: Full sun to partial shade
Salt Tolerance: Moderate
Propagation: Seeds or root cuttings

If you have a citrus tree in your yard, then you already have a larval food source for the giant swallowtail. The native Hercules' club is also a good choice for feeding butterflies, but put it out of the way. It has sharp thorns on the trunk as well as the branches. Although a fast grower, Hercules' club doesn't get very large and can be pruned to keep it shrub-like. It is also known as southern prickly-ash, and as "toothache tree" because its fragrant leaves and bark were once used to help numb the pain of toothache. Small, off-white to pale, greenish-yellow blooms appear during the spring and early summer.

Pipevine Swallowtail ~ *Battus philenor*

Family: Swallowtail (Papilionidae)
Size: 2.0" to 4.5"
Range: All of Florida north of Fort Myers
Season of Flight: Spring to Fall
Preferred Habitat: Open fields, gardens.
Adult Life Expectancy: 1 to 2 weeks
Larval Foods: Pipevines (*Aristolochia* spp.)

© ROBIN COLE/COLEPHOTO

Once a predator has tasted a pipevine swallowtail butterfly, chances are he won't go back for more. The caterpillars consume plant toxins in their larval food, and these are stored in the body of the adult butterfly. These poisons are so potent that some birds will throw up after making the mistake of trying to eat either a caterpillar or an adult. Many butterflies take advantage of this predatory defense through mimicry, including the female black swallowtail, the red-spotted purple, and the spicebush swallowtail.

IDENTIFICATION: The upper wings of the adult butterfly are smoky black and shimmering blue, with white spots dotting the edges of the wings. The underside is chocolate brown with a few creamy-white spots on the forewing. The underside of the hindwing has large orange marks ringed in black on a field of shimmering blue, with the center chocolate brown. Females are normally larger, while males are brighter and more colorful. Dark orange eggs are laid in groups, but when the spiny black caterpillars hatch, they head off on their own. The caterpillars are purplish-black with pairs of fleshy protuberances along the back that are tipped in deep reddish-orange. Another pair on the head is extra long and black in color. The chrysalis is olive brown and resembles a leaf. It is anchored to the twig by its base and is supported by a silken girdle.

Polydamas Swallowtail
Battus polydamas

Family: Swallowtail (Papilionidae)
Wingspan: 3.0" to 4.5"
Range: Peninsular Florida (more common in coastal areas)
Season of Flight: Late spring to mid-fall
Preferred Habitat: Gardens, piney woods, old fields
Adult Life Expectancy: 1 to 3 weeks
Larval Foods: Pipevines *(Aristolochia* spp.)

© ROBIN COLE/COLEPHOTO

Although the polydamas (or gold rim) swallowtail is a member of the family Papilionidae, it lacks the "tails" on the hindwings that characterize other members of the family. Like the pipevine swallowtail, polydamas caterpillars and adults are protected by the toxins present in their larval food, pipevines.

IDENTIFICATION: The underside of the polydamas swallowtail is chocolate brown, with orange dashes along the outer edges of the hindwings, and pale yellow on the wing margins. The upper side of the wings is sooty black, with a wide, broken, yellow band running along the rear part of the fore- and hindwings. The wing edges are marked with narrow scallops of yellow. The underside of the abdomen has reddish-orange longitudinal stripes along each side. I had just set a pot containing a

© JOHN & GLORIA TVETEN/KAC PRODUCTIONS

pipevine out on my deck when a polydamas swallowtail appeared and began to lay eggs on it. Shortly thereafter, unknown to me, a pipevine swallowtail followed suit. When the eggs hatched (9 polydamas and 7 pipevines) the differences quickly became apparent. Polydamas caterpillars are brownish-red with orange stripes and orange, fleshy tubercles, while pipevine caterpillars are black, with red and black tubercles. Polydamas eggs are reddish-brown, with a bumpy surface. The chrysalis may be brown or green.

53

© JAN ALLYN

Pipevines ~ *Aristolochia* spp.

Family: Birthwort (Aristolochiaceae)
Plant Type: Climbing vine
Florida Zones: N, C, S
Soil: Well-drained
Water: Moderately drought tolerant once
    established.
Light: Varies; full sun to light shade
Mature Size (H x W): to 30 ft. high
Salt Tolerance: Varies; low to moderate
Flowering Season: Summer, for most species
Propagation: Seed

Pipevines are named for the strange, pipe-shaped "flowers" that appear beginning the second year. The flower (actually a calyx having no petals) is usually a cream color marked with mottled purple or greenish-brown. Some species have unpleasant-smelling flowers. Most pipevines lose their deep green, heart-shaped leaves each winter. Vigorous climbers, they may require pruning during summer to prevent their becoming rampant. Twining and turning, seeking the light, pipevines can take intense munching dished out by hordes of pipevine and polydamas swallowtail caterpillars. They can be grown from seed, either started in pots and transplanted to the ground, or maintained in pots.

Marsh's Dutchman's pipe (*A. pentandra*) is a small-flowered, native species endemic to hammocks of south Florida and the West Indies. It is evergreen and blooms year-round. Woolly pipevine (*A. tomentosa*) is native to the Florida Panhandle and points north, growing in moist forests. It has small, greenish or purplish flowers and fuzzy leaves. Virginia snakeroot (*A. serpentaria*) is a small-leaved, low-growing, deciduous perennial that occurs most often in central and north Florida. Dutchman's pipe (*A. maxima*) has large flowers and is cultivated widely. A native of tropical America, it may be grown in frost-free areas of central and south Florida. Pelican flower (*A. grandiflora*) has huge, maroon-and-cream flowers that smell bad—but only the first day they are open. Both are tropical exotics. Nonnative pipevines are potentially invasive, so it is preferable to keep them contained in pots.

Zebra Swallowtail
Eurytides marcellus

Family: Swallowtail (Papilionidae)
Wingspan: 2.25" to 4"
Florida Range: Statewide, except southeastern coast and Florida Keys
Season of flight: Early spring through December
Preferred Habitat: Open woodlands near larval food
Adult Life Expectancy: 1 to 2 weeks
Larval Foods: Pawpaws (*Asimina* spp.)

© BETTY WARGO

This butterfly's long, elegant tails and zebra-like stripes make it easy to identify. Despite the fact that its range includes much of the eastern U.S., the zebra swallowtail is often a challenge to attract to your garden. The only place you'll see them is near their host plant, the pawpaw. Pawpaws are native plants whose habitat is being gobbled up by suburban sprawl. So imagine my excitement when, in very urban Pinellas county, I saw a whole crowd of zebra swallowtails flitting peacefully among tall grass on a vacant lot. Thrilled, I swerved off the road for a closer look. Walking out among the butterflies, I realized that I had stumbled upon a huge stand of pawpaw. The lot was also full of other Florida native plants like redroot (*Lachnanthes* spp.), sand blackberry (*Rubus cuneifolius*), St. Peter's wort (*Ascyrum* spp.), and false foxglove (*Agalinis purpurea*). I contacted the owner of the property and got permission to visit, which I did often. Sadly, the property has since been sold and a motel now occupies the site. All I have left to remember this urban oasis are the photographs I took there.

IDENTIFICATION: Adults have long, black tails tipped with white. Wings have prominent, vertical, white or greenish-white stripes. A bright red spot marks the upper side of the hindwing. The underside of the hindwing has a red stripe extending from the leading to the trailing edge, with red and blue spots at its base. The size varies because the first broods of the spring usually produce the smallest butterflies of the season, but more butterflies are born then. The largest zebra swallowtails can be seen in late fall and early winter. Caterpillars have yellow and white bands on a background that changes from light green to smoky black as they grow. Eggs are green, and the pale green chrysalis resembles a folded leaf.

Pawpaws ~ *Asimina* spp.

Family: Custard apple (Annonaceae)
Plant Type: Small to medium-sized shrub or
    small tree
Florida Zones: Varies with species; N, C, S
Soil: Sandy to organic, well-drained, acid
Water: Varies with species
Light: Full sun to partial shade
Mature Size (H x W): 12 inches to 35 ft.,
    depending on species
Salt Tolerance: Moderate
Propagation: Seed, with germination usually
    occurring the following season
Flowering Season: Varies with species; winter
    through spring

A. angustifolia

Pawpaws are not showy plants but they are definitely a must if you want to attract the zebra swallowtail to your garden. Because pawpaws have long tap roots, they are very difficult to transplant. It's therefore wise to prepare the garden site before you purchase plants, and not to move them once they're in the ground.

Consult a nurseryman or your local native plant society to find out which pawpaw grows best in your area. There are a variety of different species, the flowers of which are white, greenish-white, pink or maroon. Bigflower pawpaw (*A. obovata*) is native to central and south Florida, has oblong leaves, white flowers, and two- to three-inch long fruits. It may reach 12 feet in height and prefers dry, sandy soil. Narrow-leaf pawpaw (*A. angustifolia*) has leaves that are more long and narrow. Its flowers are ivory to pale yellow. It grows in north and north-central Florida and also prefers well-drained, sandy soil. Smallflower pawpaw (*A. parviflora*) has small maroon flowers and prefers a moist, fertile site in partial shade. It reaches 15 feet in height and grows in north and central Florida. Dwarf pawpaw (*A. pygmaea*), only a foot high, grows in sandy fields in central and north Florida.

The fruits of all Florida pawpaws are edible. They are small, usually only two to three inches long, and have a banana-like flavor. They are relished by wildlife.

A. pygmaea

56

SULPHUR BUTTERFLIES

Family Pieridae. Sulphur butterflies are named for their bright coloration, reminiscent of the element. The species' color varies from lemony yellow to bright orange, and pastel green to faded white. Some of the females have both a yellow and a white form. Sulphurs close their wings while basking, resting or nectaring; it is hard to catch them with their wings open except in flight. The chrysalis of many sulphur butterflies resembles a seashell and becomes transparent just before the butterfly emerges.

Cloudless Sulphur
Phoebis sennae

Family: White and sulphur
butterfly (Pieridae)
Wingspan: 2" to 3"
Florida Range: Statewide
Season of Flight: All year
Preferred Habitat: Open
fields, gardens and
beaches
Adult Life Expectancy: 5
to 10 days
Larval Food: Cassias (*Senna*
spp.) and partridge pea
(*Chamaechrista fasciculata*)

Cloudless sulphur butterflies give meaning to the word "butter-fly." They are like bits of the sun that have fallen to earth and chosen to stay. They are very common, easily enticed to gardens, and especially partial to red-flowering nectar sources. Although they are seen year-round in Florida, they are seasonal visitors to northeastern states, migrating in spring and fall. Each spring, cloudless sulphur

butterflies are a colorful sight along Florida roadsides and median strips, bits of yellow bursting from swathes of red, deep pink and white phlox flowers. Adults are skittish, constantly on the move, erratically flying from one flower to the next.

IDENTIFICATION: While males are pure yellow, female cloudless sulphurs have small black spots and markings along the edges of the forewings. Both sexes have very small, silver spots, rimmed in pink, on the undersides of the hindwings. Generally, females are not as vibrantly colored as males, with hues ranging from yellow to white. Caterpillars have a yellow stripe down the side and range from bright green to yellow. They are easy to photograph and observe, as they lie immobile on the host plant all day. Eggs change in color from white to pale orange. The chrysalis has a large hump in the middle and may be green or pink, with green or yellowish-green stripes. It becomes transparent just before the adult emerges.

Orange-Barred Sulphur
Phoebis philea

Family: White and sulphur butterfly
   (Pieridae)
Wingspan: 2" to 3"
Florida Range: Southern Florida, straying
   north
Season of Flight: All year
Preferred Habitat: Urban areas, gardens,
   anywhere their larval food is found
Adult Life Expectancy: 5 to 10 days
Larval Food: Cassias (*Senna* spp.) and par-
   tridge pea (*Chamaechrista fasciculata*)

Orange-barred sulphur butterflies are splashed with yellow and fiery orange-red, like tiny flecks of sunset. I often see them nectaring on the tiny blossoms of the equally fiery tropical sage. Strong fliers, they visit gardens but are often seen flitting along at treetop-level. They are very active, fidgety butterflies that seldom stay in one place for long and dart away at the first hint of a shadow. As they nectar and bask in the sun with wings closed, you are more likely to see the underside of their wings than the upper side. To keep sulphurs coming back to your garden, plant nectar sources that produce bright red flowers, such as tropical sage (*Salvia coccinea*) and red pentas (*Pentas lanceolata*). Add a few species of cassia, their larval food, and you will soon spot dashes of sunset color flitting among your flowers.

IDENTIFICATION: Male orange-barred sulphurs are a deep orange-yellow above, with striking orange bars across the forewings. The female's coloration is similar, but paler, and she has small black spots along the outer edges of fore- and hind-wings. Both sexes have a dusting of orange on the upper side of the hindwings. The undersides of the wings are yellow-orange with small brown spots. The vibrant-colored caterpillars may be yellow or green with a dark stripe down the middle and tiny black knobs all over. During its last instar, however, this caterpillar changes to a bright yellow. The chrysalis has a large "hump" in the middle and is attached to its support by a silk pad at the tip and a silk "lasso" around its middle. When the adult is ready to emerge, the case breaks open close to the head and the crinkled butterfly appears. Eggs are a translucent, creamy white at first, turning orange.

Bahama Cassia
Senna mexicana var. *chapmanii*

Family: Pea (Fabaceae)
Plant Type: Woody perennial
Florida Zones: C, S
Soil: Sandy to organic
Water: Drought tolerant after
    establishment
Light: Full sun to partial shade
Salt tolerance: High
Mature Size (H x W): 10 ft. x 5 ft.
Flowering Season: Year-round.
Propagation: Seed

Bahama cassia is a flowering shrub or small tree with bright green, oval leaflets about $3/4$" in length. It has a rather narrow trunk and smooth, yellowish-brown bark. Lemon yellow blossoms cover the tree in late summer through winter, attracting sulphur butterflies eager to deposit their eggs. As evening arrives, the tree's leaflets fold together tightly. Bahama cassia is a lovely specimen plant even when it's not blooming. Though it can be grown in central Florida, it must be protected from cold, as it will freeze back to the ground or be killed outright by frosty weather. It benefits from a light application of organic fertilizer monthly during its blooming period. Plant Bahama cassia next to a bed of red pentas for a striking color combination. Periodically prune lower limbs during the growing season to give this plant a treelike shape.

Partridge Pea ~ *Chamaecrista fasciculata*

Family: Pea (Fabaceae)
Plant Type: Annual wildflower
Florida Zones: N, C, S
Soil: Sandy, well-drained, acid
Water: Drought tolerant after establishment
Light: Full sun
Mature Size (H x W): 3 ft. x 2 ft.
Salt tolerance: High
Flowering Season: Spring–fall
Propagation: Seed

© JAN ALLYN

Partridge pea is an annual wildflower naturally found in dry, sandy, acid soil in sandhill pinelands. It thrives in these barren conditions and is also seen growing along roadsides and in disturbed areas.

It has feathery leaves and reddish stems, with showy, five-petalled, yellow flowers that grow along the leaf stalks. Sow seeds in several different open, sunny areas. Wider dispersal will increase the chances of butterfly visitation and caterpillar survival. Thin plants after they appear in late spring, leaving about two feet between them.

© DALE McCLUNG

Privet Cassia ~ *Senna ligustrina*

Family: Pea (Fabaceae)
Plant Type: Evergreen shrub
Florida Zones: C, S
Soil: Sandy to loamy, well-drained
Water: Moderately drought tolerant after establishment
Light: Full or partial sun
Mature Size (H x W): 6 ft. x 2 ft.
Salt tolerance: High
Flowering Season: All year
Propagation: Seed

Privet cassia is native to hammocks of central and south Florida and the West Indies. It has shiny green, compound leaves, attractive yellow flowers and flat seed pods that grow to be about five inches long. Essentially a plant of the tropics, it may be damaged by frost. For this reason, central Florida gardeners should put this plant in a protected location.

GOSSAMER-WINGED BUTTERFLIES

Family: Lycaenidae (Gossamer-wings); Subfamily: Theclinae (Hairstreaks).
Gossamer means something light, delicate, sheer. The tiny butterflies in this family were possibly named for the brilliant, shimmery color most have on their upper wings. The butterflies in the subfamily hairstreak have a row of pale-colored spots or a thin "hairstreak" line that marks the underside of the hind- and forewings. If you look closely, you can also see that their antennae are striped. Most butterflies in this subfamily have tails that distract predators, pointing them to the wing, instead of the much more important head.

Atala ~ *Eumaeus atala*

Family: Gossamer-wings
  (Lycaenidae)
Wingspan: 1.5" to 2.0"
Florida Range: Extreme south-
  eastern Florida
Season of Flight: All year
Preferred Habitat: Hammocks,
  edges of woods
Adult Life Expectancy: 3 to
  10 days

© MICHAEL TURCO

Pressured by loss of habitat and the shrinking availability of its larval food plant the coontie, the atala butterfly was once thought to be extinct in Florida. But its population has recovered, thanks to widespread use of coontie as a landscape plant and to the actions of concerned conservationists. Atalas fly close to the ground at a leisurely pace. They are picky in choosing their nectar plants, preferring the flowers of lantana (*Lantana* spp.) and Spanish needle (*Bidens pilosa*).

IDENTIFICATION: The atala is easily recognized by its bright red abdomen. The upper side of its black wings vary slightly in the male and female. Males are dusted with shimmering blue-green, while females are more blue. The wings of both sexes have metallic blue spots on the undersides, as well as a bright, orange-red patch next to the coral-red abdomen. The caterpillars are also red, and have seven pairs of distinct yellow dashes. They have voracious appetites, so make sure to plant several coonties if you plan to provide for atalas. Eggs are usually laid in groups; they are white, oblong with a depression in the top, and have a slightly bumpy surface. Like the caterpillar, the chrysalis is brick red.

© JAN ALLYN

Coontie ~ *Zamia pumila*

Family: Cycad (Cycadaceae)
Plant Type: Herbaceous perennial
Florida Zones: C, S
Soil: Well drained, sandy with some organic material
Water: Drought tolerant after establishment
Light: Full sun to shade
Salt Tolerance: Moderate
Mature Size (H x W): 1.5 ft. x 3.0 ft.
Flowering Season: Coontie does not flower, instead produces a seed cone
Propagation: Seed

The shining, fern-like fronds of coontie add a tropical look to the garden.
Members of the cycad family, to which coontie belongs, have been around since
dinosaurs roamed the earth. These interesting plants are stunning planted on a
mound, and are often used as an attractive ground cover. Like many other larval
food plants, coontie contains poisonous compounds that are transferred first to
the caterpillar, then to the adult butterfly. These natural toxins help butterflies
repel their enemies. The seeds are also poisonous. Look for atala eggs on the ten-
der new growth. Although the natural range of coontie extends to central
Florida, atala butterflies are residents of southeastern Florida, with an occasional
stray as far north as Indian River County. Coontie can be propagated from seed,
but because it grows so slowly, it is best to purchase enough container-grown
plants to fill your allotted garden space. It can take four years or more for nurs-
ery-grown specimens to reach salable size. Coontie is on the Florida Department
of Agriculture's list of Commercially Exploited Plants.

SKIPPER BUTTERFLIES

Skippers have large, hairy bodies, small wings and huge eyes. Their antennae look like long clubs with hooks on the ends. The source of the common name "skipper" is obvious to anyone who has spent time watching these butterflies. They flit to and fro in a constant stream of motion, appearing to skip from flower to flower. Their caterpillars make a nest for themselves out of silk and the leaves of their host plant. Most pupate inside the nest and emerge as adults.

Long-tailed Skipper
Urbanus proteus

Family: Skipper butterfly
  (Hesperidae)
Wingspan: 1.5" to 2.0"
Florida Range: Statewide
Season of Flight: All year
Preferred Habitat: Gardens and
  woodland edges
Adult Life Expectancy: 10 to 15 days
Larval food: Various members of the
  legume and mustard families, includ-
  ing wisteria (*Wisteria frutescens*)
  and butterfly pea (*Centrosema
  virginianum*), garden beans, beg-
  gar weed (*Desmodium* spp.)

Most skippers are small and drab compared to flashier butterflies like the swallowtails. Skippers have large, hairy bodies and much smaller wings than members of other butterfly families. They move with bullet speed, "skipping" quickly from flower to flower. In my yard, the population of long-tailed skippers increased rapidly after I planted a large patch of green beans, one of their favorite larval foods.

© JAN ALLYN (both)

IDENTIFICATION: The long-tailed skipper is easily recognized by its long tails and shimmering blue-green scales on its back and wings. The tails of this dusky brown skipper are often as long as its entire body. The underside of the wings is silvery-white, marked with small white spots. Caterpillars are light green with yellow or orange stripes, black stripes, and a reddish-brown head. Eggs are very pale yellow. The chrysalis is dark brown, with yellow and blue tints and a powdery white surface.

American Wisteria
Wisteria frutescens

Family: Pea (Fabaceae)
Plant Type: Woody, deciduous vine
Florida Zones: N, C
Soil: Rich, organic
Water: Moist site or regular irrigation
Light: Part shade to full sun
Mature Size: 30 feet in length or more
Salt Tolerance: Moderate
Flowering Season: Spring and summer
Propagation: Cuttings

Wisteria's springtime shower of fragrant, lavender blossoms is reason enough to plant it in your garden. Whether draped along a fence or over an arbor, this twining plant is stunning when in bloom. Because this native American species doesn't produce rampant growth as Asian cultivars do, it is much easier to maintain. The flowers appear in clusters after the dark green leaves appear. I have a wisteria vine in my backyard, and the skippers knew it was there before I did, visiting it to lay eggs. It grows on a fence near the compost pile and is apparently quite old, as parts of its stem are over an inch in diameter. I haven't bothered to fertilize or to prune it, it blooms year after year, bringing me pleasure and providing larval food for the long-tailed skippers that visit.

Butterfly Pea ~ *Centrosema virginianum*

Family: Pea and bean (Fabaceae)
Plant Type: Herbaceous, perennial, twining vine
Florida Zones: N, C, S
Soil: Sandy, well-drained, acid
Water: Moderately drought tolerant
Light: Full sun to partial shade
Mature Size: 12 inches high
Salt Tolerance: Low
Flowering Season: Spring through fall
Propagation: Seeds

The unusual flower of this vine is pale lavender in color. Its round, black seeds are borne in a long, flattened pod. A good use of butterfly pea in a landscape setting is to plant it along a fence, where it can climb, with other low-growing plants in front of it. Although butterfly pea flowers best in open, sunny areas it will also tolerate filtered shade. The related pineland butterfly pea (*C. arenicola*) is listed as endangered by the Florida Department of Agriculture, and is found only in central Florida sandhill habitats. Its flowers are smaller, but otherwise it is very similar to *C. virginianum.* Keep your eyes open for seeds at your local Florida Native Plant Society meetings, as this plant is unlikely to be found at nurseries.

Cassius blue — *Leptotes cassius*

Checkered white — *Pontia protodice*

Gray hairstreak —
Strymon melinus

OTHER FLORIDA BUTTERFLIES

COMMON NAME LARVAL FOOD(S)	SCIENTIFIC NAME FLORIDA ZONE(S)
American snout Hackberry	*Libytheana carinenta* N, C
Bartram's scrub-hairstreak Woolly croton	*Strymon acis* S
Cassius blue Plumbago, legumes	*Leptotes cassius* C, S
Ceraunus blue Indigobush, other legumes	*Hemiargus ceraunus* N, C, S
Checkered white Mustard family plants	*Pontia protodice* N, C, S
Dainty sulphur Spanish needle, sneezeweed	*Nathalis iole* N, C, S
Fiery skipper Grasses, including St. Augustine and Bermuda grass, crabgrass	*Hylephila phyleus* N, C, S
Gray hairstreak Mallows and Legumes	*Strymon melinus* N, C, S
Great southern white Pepper grass, saltwort	*Ascia monuste* N, C, S
Hackberry emperor Hackberry	*Asterocampa celtis* N, C, S
Little metalmark Thistles	*Calephelis virginiensis* N, C, S
Little yellow Partridge pea, wild sensitive plant	*Eurema lisa* N, C, S
Mangrove skipper Red mangrove	*Phocides pigmalion* S

COMMON NAME LARVAL FOOD(S)	SCIENTIFIC NAME FLORIDA ZONE(S)
Mourning cloak Willow, elm, hackberry	*Nymphalis antiopa* N
Large orange sulphur Blackbead, cassias	*Phoebis agarithe* S
Pearl crescent Asters	*Phyciodes tharos* N, C, S
Red-banded hairstreak Sumac, wax myrtle	*Calycopis cecrops* N, C, S
Red-spotted purple Willow, cherry, plum, hawthorn, oak	*Limenitis astyanax* N, C
Ruddy daggerwing Figs	*Marpesia petreus* C, S
Sleepy orange Cassias, clovers	*Eurema nicippe* N, C, S
Soldier White vine	*Danaus eresimus* S
Southern dogface False indigo, clover	*Colias cesonia* N, C, S
Southern hairstreak Oaks	*Satyrium favonius* N, C, S
Tawny emperor Hackberry	*Asterocampa clyton* N, C
Tropical checkered skipper Indian hemp, broomweed	*Pyrgus oileus* N, C, S
Variegated fritillary Passionvine, violets	*Euptoieta claudia* N, C, S
White M Hairstreak Oaks	*Parrhasius m-album* N, C, S

Nectar Plants

Choosing and Growing Nectar Plants

Nectar is the fuel of adult butterflies. They drink the sweet fluid produced by flowers, sipping it through a long, straw-like proboscis. In return, they help to pollinate plants. They do this by inadvertently collecting pollen as they feed. Then, as the butterfly sups from the next flower, some of the pollen is deposited there. The interdependence of plant and animal is once again made manifest.

Brightly colored, nectar-laden plants attract butterflies to your garden, but they will also be appreciated by you-for their aesthetic value. You'll discover that many of your favorites are preferred by the butterflies as well. Add some larval plants and your fluttering visitors may take up residence.

Monarch on blazing star
(Liatris spicata)

Butterflies are apparently able to see colors well beyond the range visible to human beings. The ability to see in the ultraviolet spectrum is critical in helping butterflies choose their food plants and their mating partners. Different species of butterflies seem to prefer different colors. Therefore, the wider the variety of colors of your nectar plants, the more different butterflies you will have the opportunity to attract. To provide a welcome mat for them, and a lovely garden to boot, plant as many brightly-colored flowers throughout your yard as room and finances will allow.

Extending the bloom time of your flowers is desirable, as this increases the supply of nectar for butterflies and encourages them to visit. "Deadheading" is one way to do this, and is simply removing spent or faded blossoms. Plants are programmed to reproduce themselves, so if blossoms are removed before seeds have a chance to form, most plants respond by producing more

Gray hairstreak *(Strymon melinus)* on snow squarestem *(Melanthera nivea)*

flowers to try again. Carrying a small pair of hand scissors or pruning shears on your garden strolls makes this task easy, and it's a great way to relax after a rough day at work.

Butterflies are active year-round in much of Florida. For this reason, it is important to provide a supply of nectar during each season, so pay special attention to the flowering period of the plants you choose. Select at least three different species that will blossom simultaneously for each season, as well as a supply of year-round bloomers. Many nectar plants bloom all year, but some, like blazing star (*Liatris* spp.) and cardinal flower (*Lobelia cardinalis*), go completely dormant, dying back to the ground. To fill the empty spots they leave, keep some continuously-blooming nectar plants growing in pots. When a seasonal plant dies back, insert a pot full of fresh blooming flowers in its place, remembering to remove the temporary placeholder before the growing season of the dormant plant begins. This will keep the butterflies happily nectaring, and your garden will be attractive spring, summer, fall and winter.

For optimum growth, ease of care and water conservation, group plants according to their sunlight, soil and moisture needs. The first of these, sunlight, is important to both plants and butterflies. Because butterflies require plenty of sunlight, it's best to locate the main part of your garden in the sunniest area of your yard. Map out the exposure of the sun on your landscape,

Honeycombhead *(Balduina angustifolia)*

remembering that it changes throughout the year. Use this map as a guide when planning your flower beds, choosing your nectar sources and deciding where to put them. Also, consider placing taller plants against a fence or wall, or at the center or rear of flowerbeds, so their shadows won't interfere with shorter plants' growth. It's not necessary to have a totally sunny yard to attract butterflies. In the shady areas of my yard, I grow firebush (*Hamelia patens*) and pentas (*Pentas lanceolata*) which are often visited by butterflies.

Next, consider your soil. For simplicity's sake, in the plant descriptions throughout this book, I have characterized soil as "sandy," "loamy," or "organic." Sandy soil is rough to the touch, coarse with large particles, and usually very well drained. Loamy soil is a crumbly mixture of sand, clay and some organic material; it usually retains moisture fairly well. Organic soil is rich, made up of lots of organic material such as naturally decomposed leaf litter, compost, cow manure, et cetera. To get a general idea of the type of soil prevalent in your area, consult a USDA soil survey map, usually available at your local Cooperative Extension Service office. To check your soil's pH level (0 being the most acid, 7 being neutral, and 14 being the most alkaline), collect two tablespoons of soil from a dozen different spots throughout your yard or garden area, placing it all together in a single plastic bag. Take or send the sample to your Cooperative Extension Service office or nursery for testing. I have found that it is easier to work with what you have than to try and grow plants not suited for your soil. If you have highly alkaline or acidic soil, adjust your plant choices accordingly.

To determine whether your soil is well-drained, wait until after a good hard rain, then dig a number of holes in the area in question, about a foot or so deep, and fill them with water. If it drains out within one hour, you most likely have well-drained soil. If the water is still sitting several hours later, use plants that can tolerate moisture or create a well-drained site. One way to create a well-drained site is to elevate the planting area by building a raised bed. Mix builder's sand or perlite into your soil and then do the drainage test again, adding more sand or perlite until the water drains out in 30 minutes.

Blackbead *(Pithecellobium keyense)*

Even if you are only planting a small bed, I recommend either machine- or hand-tilling your soil to a depth of at least two feet. This breaks up compacted soil, allowing roots freedom to grow and helping drainage. If you don't have a tiller (and who does in suburbia?) you can rent one, as I did, from a local truck rental place. You will reap huge rewards from this simple step, in the form of healthy, magnificent plants.

Water conservation should be the goal of every Floridian. Luckily, water use in the garden is within our power to control. Grouping plants according to their water needs is essential for two reasons. One, it cuts down on waste by directing precious water only where it is needed. Two, it prevents plants from suffering the damaging effects of over- or underwatering. For instance, cardinal flower, buttonbush and swamp sunflower prefer a continually moist area to thrive and blossom. In contrast, pennyroyal, partridge pea and butterfly-weed would perish under the same conditions. Keep in mind that soil drainage and amount of sunlight will also affect water needs.

Although most native plants, if planted in an environment similar to their natural habitat, can survive on rainfall alone, all plants require additional water until they become established. Very important questions to ask your nurseryman are: "How long does this plant take to establish?" and "How often should it be watered during this time?" Also ask "What are the long-term water needs of this plant?" Don't set yourself up for failure-ask these questions!

Even well-established plants require additional water during times of extreme drought. Many plants droop slightly during the hottest part of the day, but if a plant still looks stressed early in the morning, it probably needs water. Adding a light layer of mulch, such as leaves or pine needles, will help stop excessive surface evaporation. Apply a slightly thicker layer of mulch around water lovers. Around perennials that die back to the ground each year (blazing star, some goldenrods, elephant's foot, for example) make certain that mulch is not heavy enough to smother new growth.

Tropical sage
(*Salvia coccinea*)

If you would like to grow some of the moisture-loving plants but don't have any wet spots, you can create a simple bog area for them. Begin by digging a hole 1½ feet deep. Line the bottom and sides with an old shower curtain or heavy plastic sheeting, poking holes in the plastic every two feet with scissors. Next, spread a layer of small stones on the bottom. Fill the rest of the hole with dirt, compost, and other organic matter up to five inches from ground level. Fill with water, wait a few days for settling, and then plant. Make sure your "bog" doesn't dry out by adding water as needed.

Stokes' aster
(*Stokesia laevis*)

It's up to you whether to start your garden from seeds or to buy established plants. Although many flowers can be grown from seed, native Florida wildflower seed sources are not always readily available. Native plant nurseries are increasing in number and variety of stock, but seeds are still hard to find. For this reason, some people collect seed from the wild, a practice that should be discouraged. Never remove a plant from the wild, except to rescue it from imminent destruction, such as on a construction site, and then always get the landowner's permission. Alternatively, buy container-grown plants whenever possible, and use your own plants as reproductive material. Propagating extra plants and sharing them with friends is one of the joys of gardening. The aim of this book is to encourage the replenishment of butterfly habitat, not its elimination by removal of seeds or plants.

At the local chapter of the Florida Native Plant Society you'll find folks who share your interests. You will enjoy their meetings and find knowledge, friends and source material. They often have plants or seeds to share, raffle or exchange. (See the back of the book for more information.) Other groups worth checking out are the Florida Federation of Garden Clubs, North American Butterfly Association, and the Xerces Society. The garden page of your local newspaper is a great source of information, often listing the meeting times of local groups interested in butterfly gardening.

A complete list of nectar plants would be longer than the space allowed in this small book. Included here is a sampling of showy nectar plants, mostly native species. They are plants that I have grown which have proven to attract butterflies. Their colors range from brilliant reds to soft lavenders and bright yellows. There are spring, summer, fall and winter bloomers, with many species that will grow statewide. Remember, providing a large spectrum of colors will assure you of the widest variety of butterflies possible, and give you a beautiful garden as well.

Black-eyed Susan
Rudbeckia hirta

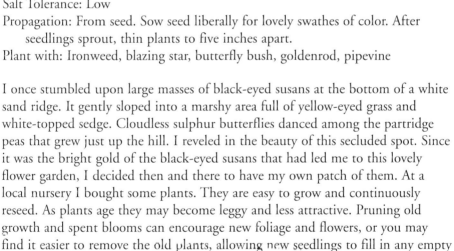

Family: Aster (Asteraceae)

Plant Type: Annual or perennial wildflower

Florida Zones: N, C, S

Mature Size (H): 2 feet

Flowering Season: Summer to fall

Soil: Sandy to slightly organic. Site must be well-drained or plants will rot; mix in sand if necessary

Water: Water until established; prefers moist, well-drained area

Light: Full sun to light shade

Salt Tolerance: Low

Propagation: From seed. Sow seed liberally for lovely swathes of color. After seedlings sprout, thin plants to five inches apart.

Plant with: Ironweed, blazing star, butterfly bush, goldenrod, pipevine

I once stumbled upon large masses of black-eyed susans at the bottom of a white sand ridge. It gently sloped into a marshy area full of yellow-eyed grass and white-topped sedge. Cloudless sulphur butterflies danced among the partridge peas that grew just up the hill. I reveled in the beauty of this secluded spot. Since it was the bright gold of the black-eyed susans that had led me to this lovely flower garden, I decided then and there to have my own patch of them. At a local nursery I bought some plants. They are easy to grow and continuously reseed. As plants age they may become leggy and less attractive. Pruning old growth and spent blooms can encourage new foliage and flowers, or you may find it easier to remove the old plants, allowing new seedlings to fill in any empty spots. Black-eyed susans make wonderful cut flowers, too.

Beach Sunflower
Helianthus debilis

Family: Aster (Asteraceae)
Plant Type: Annual or perennial
    wildflower
Florida Zones: N, C, S
Mature Size (H): 2 feet
Flowering Season: Year round
Soil: Well-drained, sandy to loamy
Water: Extremely drought tolerant
Light: Full sun
Salt Tolerance: High
Propagation: Seed, cuttings
Plant with: Blanketflower, trailing
    porterweed, seaside goldenrod,
    cassia and firebush

A great plant for coastal gardens, beach sunflower is also wonderful in other low-maintenance landscapes. Although technically an annual, it will overwinter in years with mild weather and in southern Florida. It may be damaged or even killed by freezing weather. However, a crop of new seedlings usually appears the following spring, so it's best to wait and see if this occurs before running out and buying replacement plants. The sunny yellow, daisy-like flowers have dark centers and appear throughout the growing season. Beach sunflower's rambling, vine-like habit and fast growth rate make it a perfect groundcover; it will quickly fill a flowerbed. This sunflower will grow in the poorest of soil, and is also known as dune sunflower because it often is found growing at the foot of coastal sand dunes. It is extremely tolerant of both salt spray and salty soil. If treated to warm weather, fertile soil and regular watering, it may become rampant and need frequent pruning. Once established, it will thrive on rainfall alone.

© JAN ALLYN

Blanketflower
Gaillardia pulchella

Family: Aster (Asteraceae)
Plant Type: Annual wildflower
Florida Zones: N, C, S
Mature Size (H): 10 to 12 inches
Flowering Season: Spring
    through fall
Soil: Well-drained, sandy
Water: Extremely drought tolerant
Light: Full sun
Salt Tolerance: High
Propagation: Seed
Plant with: Tropical sage, pentas, dotted horsemint, passionvine

I've known this coastal plant since childhood. Growing up in Brevard county, I loved these daisy-like flowers, red-orange with their yellow-tipped petals (or occasionally they are all yellow). It was always a happy surprise to find them popping up on the back side of the dunes. Tough guys, they require little or no care, growing in straight-up summer sun and sandy, well-drained soil. I use them for cut flowers and if I keep them trimmed with my scissors I can have blooms almost year-round. Collect seed anytime. Save the seed heads in a brown paper bag for future plantings. I've had seed sprout over a year after it was collected. To plant it, just toss seed heads on the ground and gently step on them. Seeds will sprout with minimal moisture. Pull out old, leggy plants every second year to make room for new, healthy ones. They are great for beach, coastal and seawall areas, and are a favorite nectar source of the great southern white butterfly.

Blazing Star ~ *Liatris* spp.

Family: Aster (Asteraceae)
Plant Type: Perennial wildflower
Florida Zones: N, C, S
Mature Size (H): 1 to 3 feet
Flowering Season: Late summer to fall
Soil: Well drained, acid
Water: Moderately to very drought toler-
 ant depending on species
Light: Full sun to lightly filtered shade
Salt Tolerance: Low
Propagation: Divide clumps in winter, or
 plant seeds immediately after they are
 collected.
Plant with: Ironweed, garberia, milkweed
 (*Asclepias humistrata*, *A. tomentosa*,
 A. tuberosa), partridge pea, pawpaw
 (*Asimina obovata*)

There are a number of different varieties of blazing star, sometimes called gayfeather, all pretty enough to rate a garden of their own. They appear as grass-like clumps in the spring, bloom in the summer or fall, and then die back, disappearing completely. It's a good idea to mark the spot, so you'll know where to expect them to pop up for next season's show. The long, graceful flower spikes are covered with tiny, light pink to deep purple blossoms that provide plenty of nectar. They are often used in fall flower arrangements-if you can bear to take them away from the butterflies that hang on the sides like Christmas ornaments, greedily sipping nectar. The lavender plumes are long lasting and make a striking contrast when planted with yellow flowers like goldenrod and black-eyed susan.

Butterfly Bush
Buddleia spp.

Family: Logania (Loganiaceae)
Plant Type: Woody perennial shrub
Florida Zones: N, C, S
Mature Size (H): To 15 feet
Flowering Season: Spring to fall
Soil: Fertile, loamy.
Water: Irrigate regularly to keep soil moist.
Light: Full sun to light shade
Salt Tolerance: Low
Propagation: Tip cuttings.
Plant with: Wild petunia, black-eyed susan, mistflower, milk-weed (*Asclepias viridis*), black cherry, pentas

When I brought my first butterfly bush home, the butterflies couldn't even wait for me to plant it. The same day, while it was sitting in a pot on my back deck, I watched a feisty red admiral land and do its "nectar stomp" on a drooping, lavender blossom. Butterfly bush is a must for any butterfly garden; it can't be beat as a nectar source. Although there are various colors now available-ranging from white to nearly red to midnight purple-the old "garden variety" lavenders seem to attract the most attention from nectar seekers. Give your butterfly bush a good six-foot berth and you'll be amazed at the number of different butterflies that come to visit. If you're concerned about space, choose one of the dwarf varieties, which can even be grown in a pot. Prune butterfly bush in early spring when all chance of frost has passed, as you would a favorite rose. It will rebound even if cut back to a foot tall or less, and since it blossoms on new growth it will give you even more beautiful, fragrant blooms. Apply organic fertilizer every three weeks during bloom period.

Butterfly-weed ~ *Asclepias tuberosa*

Family: Milkweed (Asclepiadaceae)
Plant Type: Perennial wildflower
Florida Zones: N, C, S
Mature Size (H): 1 to 2 feet
Flowering Season: Summer
Soil: Well-drained, sandy garden soil
Water: Water to establish, then rainfall
Light: Full sun
Salt Tolerance: Low
Propagation: Seeds
Plant with: Blazing star, elephant's foot, pennyroyal, dotted horsemint, pawpaw (*Asimina angustifolia*), butterfly pea, Florida paintbrush, twinflower, other dry-site milkweeds (*Asclepias tomentosa, A. humistrata*)

For outstanding garden color, this bright, yellow-orange to reddish-orange wildflower is hard to beat. Planted in huge masses it is especially showy, and butterflies love it. Its only major drawback is that it completely disappears when it's done blooming. It will come back each year if it is given plenty of sun and not too much water. Don't mulch heavily or water excessively, as the roots have a tendency to rot if pampered. Because it lacks the milky sap of other milkweeds, butterfly-weed makes an excellent cut flower for long-lasting bouquets. After the seed pod splits open, remove the seeds and sow them directly into a prepared garden spot. Because butterfly-weed has a long tap root, it's best not to disturb it once established.

Buttonbush
Cephalanthus occidentalis
Family: Madder (Rubiaceae)
Plant Type: Deciduous shrub
Florida Zones: N, C, S
Mature Size (H x W): 10 ft. x 5 ft.
Flowering Season: Summer and fall
Soil: Organic
Water: Moist to wet
Light: Full sun for best blooms
Salt Tolerance: Low
Propagation: Layering and tip cuttings
Plant with: Standing water – pickerelweed, water hyssop or cardinal flower; moist areas – mistflower, climbing blue aster, Florida flame azalea, water hyssop, redroot, swamp milkweed

This plant is a real treasure for a bog garden. If you have a wet area, a pond or a marsh, this dark green shrub will thrive planted on the banks or even right in the water. An attractive plant that will also grow in dryer areas, buttonbush blooms prolifically. Its fragrant, ball-shaped, white flowers attract hordes of hungry butterflies in search of nectar. It seems especially tempting to the polydamas, pipevine and other swallowtails. Plant their larval food nearby and you may entice them to take up residence and produce generations of butterflies for your enjoyment. If given enough space, buttonbush can grow to over five feet in width, eventually becoming a small tree.

Cardinal Flower
Lobelia cardinalis

Family: Bluebell (Campanulaceae)

Plant Type: Herbaceous perennial wildflower

Florida Zones: N, C

Mature Size (H): 4 ft. or more

Flowering Season: Summer, fall

Soil: Rich, loamy

Water: Moist, even occasionally
flooded sites

Light: Partial shade to full sun

Salt Tolerance: Low

Propagation: Division (spring or fall),
seed, cuttings (summer)

Plant with: Redroot, Eliott's aster, buttonbush, mistflower, water hyssop, Florida
flame azalea, climbing blue aster, coreopsis

Cardinal flower has bright scarlet flowers. You also may find cultivated varieties
that have pink or white flowers. Cardinal flower prefers a wet site, and will even
grow in shallow standing water, its natural habitat being along the margins of
streams and wetlands and in ditches. In moist, loamy soil it will withstand full
sun. Cardinal flower will tolerate sandy soil if plants are provided with regular
irrigation and placed in a partially shady location. Because each plant usually
produces a single flowerstalk, cardinal flower is more attractive if planted in
groups. In late fall or winter, after cardinal flower has finished blooming, small,
leafy rosettes form at the base of the stem. These should be kept clear of leaf litter, dirt and mulch, or the plant will die.

Climbing Aster
Aster caroliniensis

Family: Aster (Asteraceae)
Plant Type: Woody, evergreen,
    perennial vine or shrub
Florida Zones: N, C, S
Mature Size (H x W): 12 ft. x 3 ft.
Flowering Season: Fall, winter
Soil: Rich, organic
Water: Prefers moist site
Light: Full sun
Salt Tolerance: Moderate
Propagation: Seed, cuttings
Plant with: Coreopsis, mistflower,
    swamp sunflower, pentas, swamp milkweed

Climbing aster is a lovely plant for wet sites. It blooms in fall and winter when many other things are dormant. Its flowers are pale purplish pink with yellow centers, and are an inch or more in diameter. Their fragrance attracts adult butterflies, bees and other insects. Climbing aster can be made to grow on a trellis, tree or fence, or it will assume a shrubby form if no support is available to it. Although it prefers a moist site, once it is established it will do well without irrigation in all but the driest of times, if it is given rich, fertile, moisture-retentive

A. dumosus

soil. Other asters for wet areas include bushy aster (*A. dumosus*) and Elliott's aster (*A. elliottii*). The flowers of bushy aster appear from summer through winter, and vary in color from white to pale violet-blue, with yellow or reddish-yellow centers. Elliott's aster has pale lavender flowers with reddish-yellow centers that appear summer through late fall. These asters do not climb, but have slender, erect stems up to three feet in height.

© JAN ALLYN

C. leavenworthii

Coreopsis ~ *Coreopsis* spp.

Family: Aster (Asteraceae)
Plant Type: Annual or perennial
    wildflower
Florida Zones: N, C, S
Mature Size (H): To 3 feet
Flowering Season: All year, most
    prominent in spring
Soil: Sandy to organic
Water: Moist site or regular irrigation
Light: Full sun to partial shade
Salt Tolerance: Medium
Propagation: Seed collected and
    dried in a brown paper bag. This
    annual will reseed, popping up
    in the most unexpected places.
Plant with: Butterfly bush, pentas,
    phlox, climbing blue aster, red-
    root, pawpaw (*Asimina verticillata*)

There are so many species of coreopsis that there is sure to be one that will meet the needs of your butterfly garden. These buttery-yellow wildflowers appear in masses in roadside ditches and meadows every spring. Each slender, almost wispy, stalk supports a daisy-like blossom of bright yellow petals surrounding a small brown or yellow center. Coreopsis prefers a slightly damp area and will reseed freely if left alone. Arrange plants in groups so the flower stems can lean on each other for support. Although most species of coreopsis are bright yellow, the flowers of swamp coreopsis (*C. nudata*) have rosy pink petals surrounding yellow center discs. Swamp coreopsis is a north Florida wildflower.

Dotted Horsemint ~ *Monarda punctata*

Family: Mint (Lamiaceae)
Plant Type: Woody perennial
Florida Zones: N, C
Mature Size (H): 3 feet
Flowering Season: Summer to fall
Soil: Well-drained sandy or loamy soil
Water: Will survive on rainfall, but prefers some extra moisture
Light: Full sun to light shade
Salt Tolerance: High
Propagation: Seed, tip cuttings
Plant with: Blanketflower, tropical sage, firebush or trailing porterweed, pentas,
    butterfly pea

This unusual blooming member of the mint family should be used more in Florida gardens, especially in coastal or sandy areas. Each flower's dome-shaped center is surrounded by a ring of pink-spotted petals. Bloom spikes have a number of these blossoms stacked one above the other. Dotted horsemint is beautiful and virtually trouble-free.

However, it can blanket an area quickly, so keep it in check. Pinch new growth freely to encourage branching. The leaves are fragrant and the unusual flowers can be pressed and used to make note cards or other art projects. Dotted horsemint belongs to the same genus as bee balm (*M. fistulosa*), a red- or pink-flowering insect attractant that is native to the eastern United States.

Elephant's Foot ~ *Elephantopus elatus*

Family: Aster (Asteraceae)
Plant Type: Perennial wildflower
Florida Zones: N, C, S
Mature Size (H): 1 to 2 ft.
Flowering Season: Late summer, fall
Soil: Well-drained soil with moderate organic content
Water: Water until established, then rainfall
Light: Full sun to partial shade
Salt Tolerance: Low
Propagation: Seed, division
Plant with: Redroot, pawpaw (*Asimina verticillata*), milkweed (*Asclepias pedicillata*), coreopsis (*Coreopsis leavenworthii*) and black-eyed susan

This plant is so simple to grow that it can make even the most black-thumbed gardener proud. It is just one of Florida's many fall-blooming wildflowers, and deserves more widespread landscape use. Elephant's foot continually produces suckers, providing enough new plants to share with friends. Butterflies love the tiny purple blossoms that wave up at them from foot-long, hairy stalks. The flower clusters are also useful in dried arrangements because they will last for years.

© JAN ALLYN

False Dragonhead
Physostegia purpurea

Family: Mint (Lamiaceae)
Plant Type: Perennial wildflower
Florida Zones: N, C, S
Mature Size (H): 3 ft.
Flowering Season: Spring through fall
Soil: Moist, rich, slightly acid
Water: Moderate irrigation; tolerates flooding and short periods of drought
Light: Full sun to partial shade
Salt Tolerance: Low
Propagation: Seed
Plant with: Cardinal flower, redroot, mistflower, phlox, climbing blue aster

The dainty, soft flowers of false dragonhead are irresistable to butterflies. Dotted with purple, they range in color from pale pink to rose-purple. The square-stemmed flowerstalks of false drag-onhead are a giveaway to its membership in the mint family. They rise above an inconspicuous clump of pale green leaves. Some may know this wildflower as "obedient plant," as individual flowers may be repositioned with a gentle touch, and stay where they are put.

False Indigobush
Amorpha fruticosa

© JAN ALLYN

Family: Pea or bean (Fabaceae)
Plant Type: Woody flowering shrub
Florida Zones: N, C
Mature Size (H x W): 12 ft. x 12 ft.
Flowering Season: Spring and summer
Soil: Moist, rich, slightly acid
Water: Regular irrigation; tolerates
    flooding, but not drought
Light: Partial to full shade
Salt Tolerance: Low
Propagation: Seed, root cuttings
Plant with: Cardinal flower, redroot,
    climbing blue aster, Florida
    flame azalea, mistflower

This shrub is also known by the common names wild indigo and leadplant. Each flower has but one petal, but the stamens are showy. They are a very dark, reddish-purple color and are tipped by yellow-orange anthers. Though small, the flowers grow in dense spikes at the end of branches, making them more noticeable. Each seed pod has one or two seeds. This shrub is an attractive landscape plant, but its water demands make it disadvantageous for many locations. It is a larval food plant for the silver-spotted skipper, *Epargyreus clarus*, found in wet woodlands of north and central Florida, and for the southern dogface butterfly, *Colias cesonia*, found in sandhills, fields and weedy pastures throughout most of the state.

Firebush
Hamelia patens

Family: Madder (Rubiaceae)
Plant Type: Evergreen shrub
Florida Zones: C, S
Mature Size (H): 10 feet
Flowering Season: Year-round
Soil: Not very fussy, but
    grows best in well-
    drained, sandy soil
Water: Rainfall
Light: Full sun to partial
    shade
Salt Tolerance: Medium
Propagation: Tip cuttings
Plant with: Seaside golden-
    rod, tropical sage, beach
    sunflower, trailing
    porterweed

With its attractive, orange-red tinged foliage, this remarkable shrub is a garden show-off, and it's hard to overstate its value to wildlife. Tubular, nectar-filled, red flowers appear nearly year-round, and attract hummingbirds and bees as well as butterflies. Firebush also produces a continual crop of purplish fruit for the birds. The contrast of black-and-yellow striped zebras nectaring on bright red firebush flowers is simply stunning. It grows in south Florida and in coastal areas of central Florida, including my own yard. I have eight firebushes growing in both sun and partial shade, and they grow with equal vigor. The most noticeable difference is that the foliage on the plants in the shade is deeper in color. Plants in unprotected locations may die back to the ground during a hard freeze, but will come back more vigorous than ever the next spring. Allow about ten feet between plants to give them room to fill out.

Florida Flame Azalea ~ *Rhododendron austrinum*

Family: Heath (Ericaceae)
Plant Type: Deciduous shrub
Florida Zones: N, C
Mature Size (H): 15 ft.
Flowering Season: Early spring
Soil: Like other azaleas, it prefers loose, rich, very acid soil. Don't disturb the roots after it is established.
Water: Will tolerate some drought once established, but does best in moist (not mucky), well-drained soil
Light: Filtered shade
Salt Tolerance: Low
Propagation: Layering
Plant with: Mistflower, purple coneflower, ironweed (*Vernonia gigantea*), phlox

I happened upon this north Florida beauty at Maclay State Gardens near Tallahassee. Two black swallowtails drifted leisurely above the orange-yellow blossoms, stopping to nectar once or twice before spiraling upwards in a mating dance. The spicy-sweet fragrance of these flowers is attractive to butterflies and humans alike. A large, gangling azalea, it needs at least five to ten feet between plants to bloom successfully.

Florida Paintbrush ~ *Carphephorus corymbosus*

Family: Aster (Asteraceae)
Plant Type: Herbaceous perennial
Florida Zones: N, C, S
Mature Size (H): 3 feet
Flowering Season: Late summer, fall
Soil: Sandy, well-drained, acid
Water: Very drought tolerant
Light: Full sun
Salt Tolerance: Low
Propagation: Division, seeds
Plant with: Narrowleaf silkgrass, blazing star (*Liatris tenuifolia*), butterfly pea, coastalplain goldenaster, black-eyed susan, pawpaw (*Asimina obovata*)

© ROBIN COLE/COLEPHOTO

Although its blooming period is short, this wildflower has spectacular rosy-pink flower heads and is very attractive to butterflies. Its needs are slight; give it a sunny spot and a sprinkle of water now and then in times of drought. Be careful that leaf litter does not cover the basal rosette of leaves after the blooms fade. Florida paintbrush is the perfect companion plant for blazing star, as both are fall bloomers native to dry pinelands. As a lovely contrast to their pink-toned flowers, add the bright yellows of goldenaster (*Chrysopsis* spp.) and goldenrod (*Solidago* spp.). Vanilla plant (*Carphephorus odoratissima*) and deer-tongue (*C. paniculatus*) are closely related to Florida paintbrush and are also found in pinelands throughout the state. As its name implies, vanilla plant has a vanilla odor that intensifies when the plant is dried. It blooms summer through winter and likes a somewhat moist site. Deer-tongue has upright panicles of deep lavender flowers and blooms in fall to winter.

Garberia
Garberia heterophylla

Family: Aster (Asteraceae)
Plant Type: Woody perennial ever-
   green shrub
Florida Zones: N, C
Mature Size (H x W): 6 ft. x 6 ft.
Flowering Season: Summer, fall
Soil: Acid, sandy, very well drained
Water: Extremely drought tolerant
Light: Full sun
Salt Tolerance: Moderate
Propagation: Seeds or cuttings
Plant with: Pawpaw (*Asimina obo-
   vata*), blazing star (*Liatris
   chapmanii*), Florida paintbrush

© JAN ALLYN

Garberia has clusters of delicate, fragrant flowers that are so pale pink they're nearly white. This tough shrub is endemic to scrub habitats, so it has very low water and nutritional needs. Use it as a specimen shrub in a sunny spot in your yard, but don't put it near concrete foundations where alkaline soil may harm it. Garberia attracts all sorts of insects when it bursts into bloom and has attractive grayish-green leaves throughout the year. Prune it after the flowers have faded to keep it from being rangy. This plant is listed as threatened, and is endemic to the state of Florida

Goldenaster
Chrysopsis spp.
Family: Aster (Asteraceae)
Plant Type: Biennial wildflower
Florida Zones: N, C, S
Mature Size (H): 3 ft.
Flowering Season: Summer to fall
Soil: Sandy, well-drained
Water: Once established will
    exist on rainfall
Light: Full
Salt Tolerance: Moderate
Propagation: Seed
Plant with: Lantana, partridge
    pea, butterfly-weed, penny-
    royal, trailing porterweed

A bright spot in any garden, this wildflower has compact bouquets of golden blossoms at the top of each stalk. These tough guys grow best in well-drained, sandy soil and are often seen blooming in such harsh conditions as parking lots and along sidewalk edges. Their flowers seem to reflect the color of the summer sun—and the hotter it is, the more they appear to thrive. Coastalplain golden-aster is just one of over a dozen species of goldenasters that grow in Florida. Most bloom early summer through fall and prefer dry, sandy sites.

Golden Dewdrop
Duranta repens

Family: Vervain (Verbenaceae)
Plant Type: Evergreen tree or shrub
Florida Zones: C, S
Mature Size (H x W): 18 feet by 12 feet
Flowering Season: Late spring through fall
Soil: Sandy to loamy
Water: Drought tolerant once established
Light: Full sun to partial shade
Salt Tolerance: Moderate
Propagation: Cuttings
Plant with: Plant alone as a specimen, or
    in the back of the garden as a screen

Blue-flowered form

This tropical shrub has tiny, fragrant, lavender-blue or white blossoms followed by attractive, half inch-round, golden fruit. Although the berries are relished by birds, they are poisonous to people. A favorite roosting place for zebras, golden dewdrop provides cover for other butterflies as well. Give it plenty of space and it will reward you with a shower of color. Though it will tolerate shade, it blooms best in full sun. It's not fussy and will grow in just about any soil with little or no fertilizer. Plant it alongside bright red firebush for a stunning hedge. If you want a hedge, though, be vigilant with the clippers; if left unpruned, golden dewdrop will develop into a small tree. It is native to the West Indies.

© ROBIN COLE/COLEPHOTO

White-flowered form

Goldenrod ~ *Solidago* spp.

Family: Aster (Asteraceae)
Plant Type: Perennial wildflower
Florida Zones: N, C, S
Mature Size (H): 1 to 8 feet
Flowering Season: Midsummer to early winter
Soil: Does best in well-drained, sandy, acid soil
Water: Extremely drought tolerant
Light: Full sun to partial shade
Salt Tolerance: High
Propagation: Division, cuttings, seeds
Plant with: Tropical sage, pentas, Florida paintbrush, blazing star

There is simply nothing better than goldenrod to give your garden a blaze of yellow. A number of species are available, but my favorite is seaside goldenrod (*S. sempervirens*) because it is tall and it spreads quickly. Oceanside gardeners also appreciate its salt tolerance. Since goldenrods spread underground they are easily propagated by division. I have given mine its own bed so it won't infringe on other plants. Plant it in the back border of a fall garden. It is a favorite nectar source for gulf fritillaries, monarchs and other butterflies. Planted at the edge of a tree line, it will bend gracefully out towards the sun. Goldenrod has gotten a bum rap; it does not cause hay fever. Allergy sufferers are usually bothered by ragweed, which blooms at the same time. Intersperse goldenrod with blazing stars for a stunning fall display. In spite of its name and appearance, flat-topped goldenrod (*Euthamia caroliniana*) is not considered a true goldenrod. This lovely perennial is also a member of the aster family. A fall wildflower that will grow in excess of three feet, it bursts into clouds of yellow blossoms around October, and continues blooming through December. It prefers sandy, well-drained soil and full sun.

© ROBIN COLE/COLEPHOTO

Ironweed ~ *Vernonia* spp.

Family: Aster (Asteraceae)
Plant Type: Herbaceous, perennial wildflower
Florida Zones: N, C
Mature Size (H): *V. angustifolia* reaches about 3 feet in height, while *V. gigantea* may be 6 feet tall or more.
Flowering Season: Mid-summer to early fall
Soil: Slightly organic, but does fine in poor soil as well
Water: Water to establish, then only during drought
Light: Full sun to partial shade
Salt Tolerance: Moderate
Propagation: From cuttings taken in early summer, or from seeds
Plant with: Goldenrod, blazing star, black-eyed susan, butterfly bush, pentas

Ironweed blossoms are like tiny, brilliant purple paintbrushes waving at the sky. The mass of bloooms can stretch up to eight inches across. This is truly a stunning wildflower for a butterfly garden. I had no trouble establishing it in my garden, but alas, it suffered a serious accident before it produced its first bloom. A carelessly-tossed newspaper broke my plant in half. My disappointment turned into delight when two stems quickly shot up to replace the broken one. This plant responds wonderfully to pruning, so trim it anytime to keep it shapely and increase flower production. Because of its height (six feet or more) ironweed should be placed in the back of the garden.

© BILL BEATTY/COLEPHOTO

Joe-Pye-Weed
Eupatorium fistulosum
Family: Aster (Asteraceae)
Plant Type: Herbaceous perennial shrub
Florida Zones: N, C
Mature Size (H): 3 to 10 feet
Flowering Season: Late spring through fall
Soil: Fertile, loamy
Water: Drought tolerant once established, if
    planted in fertile, loamy soil
Light: Full sun to partial shade
Salt Tolerance: Low
Propagation: Seed, division
Plant with: Stokes' aster, climbing blue aster,
    butterfly bush, black-eyed susan, pentas

Because it grows quite tall, Joe-pye-weed is very nice planted at the rear of a flower garden or along a fence. Its height and lankiness contrast well with lower-growing, more rounded shrubs and groundcovers. Flowers are borne in clusters at the ends of stems and are pink to lavender. Joe-pye-weed has magenta stems, the main one being hollow, and lance-shaped leaves that have toothed edges and are spotted with purple. During the first year it requires regular irrigation, but is quite drought tolerant thereafter. Plants started from seed do not produce flowers until the second year. Store collected seed in an airtight container in the refrigerator until you are ready to sow it.

Lantana ~ *Lantana* spp.

Family: Verbena (Verbenaceae)
Plant Type: Woody perennial shrub
Florida Zones: N, C, S
Mature Size (H): 1 to 10 feet
Flowering Season: Spring to fall
Soil: Sandy to loamy, well-drained
Water: Drought tolerant
Light: Full sun
Salt Tolerance: High
Propagation: Cuttings
Plant with: Pentas, milkweed, firebush,
    tropical sage, trailing porterweed

Rockland shrubverbena
(Lantana depressa var. depressa)

Butterflies eagerly seek this shrub. Lantana's flower clusters are attractive because they have abundant nectar and their physiology makes it easy for butterflies to land on them. For fast results, put several plants in a group. Of our three native species, wild sage or button sage, *L. involucrata*, is the most prevalent. It thrives naturally in central and southern Florida, is salt tolerant, and prefers very well-drained soil. The creamy-white flowers with yellow centers are sometimes brushed with pale purple. If left undisturbed, this lantana will form a lovely thicket. Its size can be kept manageable by light pruning, if desired. Hammock shrubverbena, *L. canescens*, has white flowers, is very rare and is considered endangered. *Lantana depressa* has three varieties. All the

Weeping lantana *(Lantana montevidensis)*

flowers are usually a mixture of yellow and orange, and each leaf has a v-shaped base. Rockland shrubverbena, *L. depressa* var. *depressa* is an endangered species and very rare. Florida shrubverbena, *L. depressa* var. *floridana* occurs more often on the east coast and Sanibel shrubverbena, *L. depressa* var. *sanibelensis*, also rare, occurs along the west coast. Weeping lantana, *L. montevidensis*, is a lavender-flowered species from South America. It is low-growing and can be used as a groundcover or placed in pots throughout the garden. This lantana's light green foliage and bright flowers make a stunning border along a woodland edge. Cuttings may be taken at any time, except when the plant is dormant. Most yellow-flowered lantana found in nurseries are hybrids of native and exotic species.

Mistflower
Conoclinium coelestinum
Family: Aster (Asteraceae)
Plant Type: Perennial wildflower
Florida Zones: N, C, S
Mature Size (H): 3 feet
Flowering Season: Year round
Soil: Acid, rich, organic
Water: Prefers moist areas
Light: Full sun to partial shade
Salt Tolerance: Low
Propagation: Root division
Plant with: Buttonbush, phlox, climbing aster, black-eyed susan, pipevine

If you have room, give this blue-flowered beauty its own bed. It spreads easily and provides a lovely, deep green patch when it's not blooming. The flowers are a wonderful shade of blue and butterflies love them. They are soft, fuzzy and prolific. They strongly resemble those of cultivated ageratum, which is why mistflower is also called false ageratum. It makes a nice border and can be trimmed to fill the space available. Pinch the foliage to get bushier plants. Mistflower produces some flowers year round in southern Florida, but blooms most abundantly in fall.

Narrowleaf silkgrass ~ *Pityopsis graminifolia*

Family: Aster (Asteraceae)
Plant Type: Perennial wildflower
Florida Zones: N, C, S
Mature Size (H): 8 to 10 inches (excluding flower stems, which may be several
    feet long)
Flowering Season: Fall
Soil: Sandy, acid, well drained
Water: Water until established, then extremely drought tolerant
Light: Full sun to partial shade
Salt Tolerance: Moderate
Propagation: Divide clumps or sow seeds
Plant with: Partridge pea, Florida paintbrush, twinflower, milkweed (*Asclepias
    humistrata*), pawpaw (*Asimina angustifolia*), blazing star, butterfly-weed

I first saw this wildflower at a fall native plant sale in my area. Out of its silvery, grass-like clump of foliage an 18-inch stem burst upward, bearing branched flowerstalks with sprays of small yellow flowers. After the plant had been transplanted to my garden, the flowers lasted another week. Then, as soon as I had cut them, another stem burst into bloom. By the next spring, runners from my one plant had spread to fill an area of about a square foot. Even when its spent flowerstalks have been removed, silkgrass is attractive, its pale, silvery-green foliage providing lovely garden color. Silkgrass reseeds generously, furnishing you with plenty of sharable seedlings. Plant silkgrass at the edge of a treeline or beneath open-crowned trees where it define borders nicely.

Pennyroyal ~ *Piloblephis rigida*

Family: Mint (Labiaceae)
Plant Type: Woody perennial groundcover
Florida Zones: C, S
Mature Size (H): 8 inches
Flowering Season: Year round
Soil: Sandy, well-drained
Water: Extremely drought tolerant
Light: Full sun
Salt Tolerance: Low
Propagation: Seed, cuttings
Plant with: Twinflower, standingcypress, pawpaw (*Asimina angustifolia*), milkweed (*Asclepias tomentosa, A. humistrata*), Florida paintbrush, butterflyweed, blazing star

© JAN ALLYN

The invigorating fragrance of pennyroyal are reason enough to include it in your garden. Its minty leaves have been used to make tea and as a medicinal herb. Other points in its favor: butterflies like the flowers, it blooms sporadically throughout the year, and it thrives on complete neglect. Fertilizer is unnecessary and regular irrigation is actually a detriment, as the bright green, needle-like leaves have a tendency to rot if they stay damp for too long. My patch of pennyroyal was nearly finished off by an abnormally soggy winter. Pennyroyal's flowers are a soft lavender pink, borne in clusters at the ends of the stems. Though pennyroyal may reseed, it does not spread prolifically like some other members of the mint family. The best way to propagate it is from cuttings.

Pentas ~ *Pentas lanceolata*

Family: Verbena (Verbenaceae)
Plant Type: Evergreen shrub
Florida Zones: N, C, S
Mature Size (H): 1 to 4 feet
Flowering Season: Year round
Soil: Sandy to organic. Apply an organic fertilizer four times a year
Water: Drought tolerant after establishment
Light: Full sun to partial shade
Salt Tolerance: High
Propagation: Cuttings, anytime
Plant with: Anything in your butterfly garden, remembering that pentas
    do need room

This is possibly the best nonnative plant to have in your butterfly garden. When absolutely nothing else is blooming, these just keep on going. Prolific bloomers, they provide year-round color for you and year round nectar for your butterflies. They are so easy to grow, you cannot harm them. Simply "deadhead" them once in a while to multiply the blooms, and once or twice a year cut them back severely to keep them from becoming too leggy. I prefer the red variety because it attracts the most butterflies to my garden. There are also cultivars with pink, lavender and white flowers, as well as dwarf varieties that reach no more than a foot in height. Pentas may be damaged in a cold snap; if so, just wait until all chance of frost has passed, then prune off the dead and damaged parts of the plant. It will regrow with a vengeance.

Phlox ~ *Phlox* spp.

Family: Phlox (Polemoniaceae)
Plant Type: Annual or perennial wildflower
Florida Zones: N, C
Mature Size (H): To 1.5 feet
Flowering Season: Spring to summer
Soil: Rich, organic, loamy or sandy
Water: Drought tolerant once established
Light: Full sun to partial shade
Salt Tolerance: Low
Propagation: Cuttings, seed, clump division
Plant with: Stokes' aster, mistflower, iron-
    weed, Florida flame azalea

P. drummondii

Anyone who has traveled Florida's highways from Pinellas County northward in the springtime has been treated to a colorful rainbow of phlox. For me it is almost a pil-grimage. I head north on US Highway 19 to Maclay State Gardens to catch the wild azaleas blooming. As I ride along, I drink in the beauty provided by huge swathes of these bright blossoms. They vary in hue from white through shades of pink, blue, lavender, deep purple to near-red. A bonus is seeing yellow sulphur butterflies skip and twirl in a wondrous nectar frenzy, oblivious to the cars whizzing by. Annual garden phlox (*P. drummondii*) is nonnative, escaped from cultivation. It is one of five species of wildflowers chosen for sowing by the Florida Department of Transportation's roadside wildflower program. Trailing phlox (*P. nivalis*) is a native, woody perennial with clusters of pink flowers and needle-like leaves. Start phlox cuttings in a good rooting medium, or sow seeds between November and January (earlier in north Florida and later in south Florida).

P. nivalis

Pickerelweed ~ *Pontederia cordata*

Family: Pickerelweed (Pontederiaceae)
Plant Type: Aquatic
Florida Zones: N, C, S
Mature Size (H): 3 ft.
Flowering Season: Spring to fall
Soil: Sandy to organic
Water: Wet
Light: Full
Salt Tolerance: Low
Propagation: Division
Plant with: Cardinal flower, swamp sunflower, buttonbush, red bay, water hyssop, swamp coreopsis

Pickerelweed's lovely blue flower spikes make this aquatic wildflower worth growing. Though less common, there is also a white-flowering variety. Waterfowl eat the seeds. If you have a backyard water garden, try planting some in a shallow, submerged tub to contain its growth. It has been known to overrun small ponds. Many butterflies enjoy the nectar from its flowers.

© JAN ALLYN

Purple Coneflower
Echinacea purpurea
Family: Aster (Asteraceae)
Plant Type: Perennial wildflower
Florida Zones: N, C, S
Mature Size (H): 3 feet
Flowering Season: Summer
Soil: Organic, fertile, well-drained, alkaline
Water: Drought tolerant once established
Light: Full sun
Salt Tolerance: Moderate
Propagation: Seeds sown in fall will sprout
    the following spring
Plant with: Black-eyed susan, pentas, Stokes'
    aster, Joe-pye-weed, wild petunia

The very fragrant, nectar-rich flowers of purple coneflower must look like great landing pads to insects. Bees and butterflies descend upon them in hordes. The flower petals are actually more rose-pink than purple, sometimes reaching a full four inches across. The sturdy center "cones" are deep maroon. Often seen blooming along the roadsides during the summer, this flower can withstand drought if given some moisture until it is fully established. Water regularly at first, then only if plant shows signs of distress. Too much water may cause this plant to rot. Native coneflowers are usually taller than cultivars and can be found at many native plant nurseries. Purple coneflower makes a good cut flower and can be used in dried arrangements. It thrives in sun; if grown in shade, the color will wash out and the plant will get leggy. Purple coneflower does not do well in acid soil. Amend the soil with lime if necessary.

Redroot ~ *Lachnanthes caroliniana*

Family: Bloodwort (Haemodoraceae)
Plant Type: Perennial wildflower
Florida Zones: N, C, S
Mature Size (H): 1 to 3 feet
Flowering Season: Summer through fall
Soil: Fertile, acid
Water: Moist, even occasionally flooded
Light: Full sun
Salt Tolerance: Low
Propagation: Division of roots
Plant with: Small-flowered pawpaw (*Asimina parviflora*), coreopsis, mistflower,
     buttonbush, cardinal flower

I have seen butterflies of three different species nectaring on one redroot bloom,
all at the same time. The wide, fluffy, cream-colored blossoms of this plant are
roomy enough to share. Redroot is a wonderful addition to a butterfly garden
and it requires little more than adequate moisture during dry times. It will return
each year, its roots spreading underground to bless you with extra plants. The
leaves of redroot are flat, resembling those of iris. They are a favorite food of
sandhill cranes.

Scorpion Tail
Heliotropium angiospermum

Family: Forget-me-not
  (Boraginaceae)
Plant Type: Herbaceous perennial
Florida Zones: C, S
Mature Size (H x W): 3 ft. x 4 ft.
Flowering Season: All year
Soil: Sandy, well-drained, slightly
  alkaline
Water: Drought tolerant
Light: Full sun
Salt Tolerance: Moderate
Propagation: Seed, cuttings
Plant with: Red bay, wild lime, pas-
  sionvine, lantana, pentas

The small white flowerspikes of this heliotrope are especially attractive to blues, skippers and other small butterflies. Scorpion tail has pretty, deep-green, conspicuously veined, shiny leaves. Although it is a plant of sandy, coastal uplands, it adapts well to butterfly gardens provided the planting site has good drainage and the soil is not acid. It tends to grow out, rather than up, so it may need to be trimmed to keep it from encroaching on nearby plantings. A related species, seaside heliotrope (*Heliotropium currasavicum*) is useful in coastal landscapes because of its salt tolerance. Its leaves are more narrow and smooth, with a pale bluish cast. It also blooms all year.

Standingcypress
Ipomopsis rubra

Family: Phlox (Polemoniaceae)
Plant Type: Annual or biennial
Florida Zones: N, C
Mature Size (H): To 3 feet
Flowering Season: Summer, fall
Soil: Sandy, well-drained, not acidic
Water: Water to establish, then only
    when stress is apparent
Light: Full
Salt Tolerance: Moderate
Propagation: Seed
Plant with: Blazing star (*Liatris chap-
    manii*), elephant's foot, wild petu-
    nia, pennyroyal, butterfly pea

This north Florida wildflower requires at least six hours of sunlight. The wispy foliage is reminiscent of fennel. The tubular firecracker-red flowers also attract hummingbirds. Being one who can't resist trying a new butterfly plant, I traveled to a spring garden show at Kanapaha Botanical Gardens near Gainesville to purchase three of these plants. They don't like acid soil, so I planted them in the alkaline sand that surrounds my above-ground swimming pool. They are thriving. If your soil tends to be acid, try planting standingcypress close to the foundation of your house, where the lime from the cement sweetens the soil. Standingcypress will self-sow if the area around the plant is free from debris. This plant prefers very dry conditions, so after it's established don't water it unless it is showing stress by still drooping early in the morning.

Stokes' Aster ~ *Stokesia laevis*

Family: Aster (Asteraceae)
Plant Type: Perennial wildflower
Florida Zones: N, C, S
Mature Size (H): 1 to 1.5 feet
Flowering Season: Spring to summer
Soil: Well drained, sandy to loamy
Water: Requires regular irrigation
    and adequate drainage
Light: Full morning sun, light shade
Salt Tolerance: Low
Propagation: Seed, division
Plant with: Purple coneflower, black-
    eyed susan, butterfly bush,
    climbing blue aster, phlox

© JAN ALLYN

This perennial is easy to grow and has some very interesting traits. I have watched the flowers on mine open in the morning, then slowly close at night. Flower color ranges from white to lavender and pink. Although there may be many buds on a stem, the flowers on each stem open one at a time. The blossoms are large and inviting to most butterflies, giving them enough room to land easily. Stokes' aster is not a fussy plant and it makes a good border along a pathway or in the front of your garden. When not blooming, the basal leaves of this plant form an inconspicuous green clump. As it grows, it suckers, and new plants can be had by simple division.

Swamp Sunflower ~ *Helianthus angustifolius*

Family: Aster (Asteraceae)
Plant Type: Perennial
Florida Zones: N, C
Mature Size (H x W): 6 ft. x 2 ft.
Flowering Season: Late summer to fall
Soil: Loamy, organic
Water: Moist
Light: Full
Salt Tolerance: Moderate
Propagation: Division (spring), seed
Plant with: Swamp milkweed, cardinal flower, joe-pye-weed, climbing blue aster, Elliott's aster

© ROBIN COLE/COLEPHOTO

This blazing yellow wildflower is a must for any moist area. Line it up against a fence, intermingled with the blues of Elliott's aster and the reds of cardinal flower, for a spectacular fall display. The blossoms of swamp sunflower are exceptionally broad, up to 3 inches across, providing a nice platform on which butterflies can land and nectar. This wildflower reaches up to six feet in height, but it will die back to the ground in the winter. To mark the spot, I leave the long stems, which will turn brown and dry out. Watch for the rosettes to reappear in the spring.

Trailing Porterweed ~ *Stachytarpheta jamaicensis*

Family: Vervain (Verbenaceae)
Plant Type: Woody perennial
Florida Zones: C, S
Mature Size (H x W): 1 ft. x 5 ft.
Flowering Season: Year round
Soil: Sandy to loamy, well-drained
Water: Extremely drought tolerant once established
Light: Full sun to partial shade
Salt Tolerance: High
Propagation: From seed, gathered after the flower stems turn brown
Plant With: Blanketflower, tropical sage, passionvines, pentas, seaside goldenrod,
  firebush, bahama cassia

© JAN ALLYN

The more you ignore this plant, the better it seems to grow. I have watched it cover a five-foot area in about four months. It has lovely, deep green leaves with toothed edges, and rings of tiny blue blossoms that open up along the flower stems. It's truly amazing to watch large butterflies nectar from porterweed flowers. (Bumblebees love them, too.) They sway in the breeze, determined to extract every last drop, hanging precariously from a bloom the size of a tiny button. Each spent flower stem is a foot or more in length and can hold hundreds of seeds, providing plenty of new volunteers. This plant is an excellent choice for coastal areas and will tolerate extreme drought. Related nonnative species grow upright, reaching four feet in height, and have blue or coral pink flowers. Trailing porterweed will not withstand freezing weather, but it produces so many seedlings that the best thing to do in case of a casualty is to pull out the frost-killed parent plant and wait for new replacements to spring up.

Tropical sage
Salvia coccinea
Family: Mint (Labiaceae)
Plant Type: Annual wildflower
Florida Zones: C, S
Mature Size (H): 4 feet
Flowering Season: Year round
Soil: Sandy, well drained
Water: Water until establish, then
    rainfall is sufficient
Light: Full sun to partial shade
Salt Tolerance: High
Propagation: Seed, easily
Plant with: Goldenrod, black-eyed
    susan, blanketflower, butterfly-
    weed, pentas, bahama cassia

Tall flowerspikes of tropical sage will stand sentry over your butterfly garden. Like tiny red flags, they entice passing butterflies to stop and partake of the feast.

Enjoyed by many garden butterflies, they are also simple to grow and to propagate. They reseed freely. Pinch off spent blossoms and prune gangly branches to keep the plant bushy. I have a huge pot full of this fire-red sage on my back deck, where it allows me to observe the butterflies that feed on it. Planted with the yellows of black-eyed susan and goldenrod, it presents a really bright splash of color.

Lyre-leaved sage (*Salvia lyrata*) is another salvia that is easy to grow. Check your yard carefully; it will often show up as a volunteer. Although this perennial wildflower blooms year-round, the light purple blossoms appear most profusely in spring.

S. lyrata

Verbena ~ *Glandularia* spp.

Family: Vervain (Verbenaceae)
Plant Type: Perennial wildflower
Florida Zones: C, S
Mature Size (H): Varies with species
Flowering Season: All year (*G. maritima*), spring–fall (*G. tampensis*)
Soil: sandy, well-drained
Water: Water until established, then occasionally as needed
Light: Partial shade to full sun
Salt Tolerance: Moderate to high
Propagation: Cuttings, seed
Plant with: *G. maritima*—blanketflower, beach sunflower, pentas, tropical sage.
    G. tampensis—pentas, mistflower, butterfly bush, coreopsis

G. tampensis

Two members of the vervain or verbena family, coastal vervain (*G. maritima*) and Tampa vervain (*G. tampensis*), are great additions to a butterfly garden. Butterflies are readily attracted to the clusters of flat-topped blossoms that grow in some of our harshest environments. These lovely native wildflowers are both considered to be endangered by the Florida Department of Agriculture, which is all the more reason to plant them. Coastal vervain is a dune plant and grows most frequently on the east coast. It has lavender-pink flowers and blooms year-round. It is a low-growing plant that spreads outward to cover an area. Tampa vervain bears its deep rose-purple blossoms from spring to fall. It will grow best in partial shade and does require extra moisture from time to time. This plant is nice as a border, but can get as tall as 24 inches. It will also grow well in pots. Placing pots full of Tampa vervain on pedestals throughout your garden will add interest and a nice splash of color.

OTHER NECTAR PLANTS

COMMON NAME* LARVAL PLANT?	BLOOMING SEASON**	SCIENTIFIC NAME FULL/PART SUN	ZONE(S)
Blackbead		*Pithecellobium keyense*	
yes	F–Sp	full/part	S
Blackberry		*Rubus* spp.	
no	Sp	full	N, C
Clover		*Trifolium* spp.	
yes	Sp	full	N, C, S
Coral honeysuckle		*Lonicera sempervirens*	
no	Sp–F	full/part	N, C
French marigold*		*Tagetes patula*	
no	Sp–Su	full	N, C, S
Frog-fruit		*Phyla nodiflora*	
yes	Y	full	N, C, S
Hibiscus		*Hibiscus* spp.	
no	Y	full	N, C, S
Honeycombhead		*Balduina angustifolia*	
no	Sp–Su	full	N, C, S
Lyonia		*Lyonia* spp.	
no	Sp	full	N, C, S
Mexican sunflower*		*Tithonia rotundifolia*	
no	Sp–Su	full	N, C, S
New Jersey tea		*Ceanothus americanus*	
no	Sp	full	N, C
Rayless sunflower		*Helianthus radula*	
no	Su-F	full–part	N, C, S
Plumbago*		*Plumbago auriculatus*	
yes	Sp–F	full	C, S
Saw palmetto		*Serenoa repens*	
no	Sp–Su	full–part	N, C, S
Seaside heliotrope		*Heliotropium curassavicum*	
no	Y	full	C, S

OTHER NECTAR PLANTS *(continued)*

COMMON NAME LARVAL PLANT?	BLOOMING SEASON	SCIENTIFIC NAME FULL/PART SUN	ZONE(S)
Sedum		*Sedum spectabile*	
yes	F–W	full	N, C, S
Snapdragon*		*Antirrhinum majus*	
yes	Sp–Su	full	N, C
Snow squarestem		*Melanthera nivea*	
no	Y	full/part	N, C, S
Strawflower*		*Helichrysum* spp.	
no	Sp–Su	full	N, C
Summer farewell		*Dalea* spp.	
yes	Su–F	full	N, C, S
Sunflowers*		*Helianthus* spp.	
no	Sp–F	full	N, C, S
Sweet william*		*Dianthus* spp.	
no	Sp–Su	full	N, C
Tarflower		*Befaria racemosa*	
no	Sp–F	full	N, C, S
Thistles		*Cirsium* spp.	
no	Sp–Su	full	N, C, S
Thyme*		*Thymus* spp.	
no	Sp–Su	full–part	N, C, S
Viburnum		*Viburnum* spp.	
no	Su	full–part	N, C, S
White vine		*Sarcostemma clausum*	
yes	Y	full–part	C, S
Yarrow*		*Achillea* spp.	
no	Sp	full	N, C
Zinnias*		*Zinnia* spp.	
no	Sp–F	full	N, C, S

*   Common name followed by asterisk (*) indicates nonnative plant.

** Sp=spring, Su=summer, F=fall, W=winter, Y=year-round

PUBLIC BUTTERFLY GARDENS IN FLORIDA

BRIGGS NATURE CENTER: 401 Shell Island Road, Naples, 34113, (941)775-8569. Butterfly garden open Monday through Saturday 9:00 a.m. to 4:30 p.m.; also Sundays 1:00–4:00 p.m. during January–March.

BUTTERFLY WORLD: Tradewinds Park, 3600 W. Sample Rd., Coconut Creek, 33073, (954)977-4400. www.butterflyworld.com. The original butterfly house, the first in the United States. Indoor and outdoor gardens, plants available for purchase. Breeding lab, two-story, walk-through aviary.

CYPRESS GARDENS: State Road 540, Winter Haven, 33884, (800)237-4826. www.cypressgardens.com. "Wings of Wonder," an enclosed, walk-through conservatory featuring native and tropical butterflies. Surrounded by outside gardens planted to attract native butterflies.

KANAPAHA BOTANICAL GARDENS: 4625 Southwest 63rd Blvd., Gainesville, (352)372-4981. One and a half-mile paved walkway through gardens, picnic facilities. Closed Thursdays.

MUSEUM OF SCIENCE AND INDUSTRY: 4801 East Fowler Ave., Tampa, (813)987-6300. "Butterfly Encounter," a free-flight butterfly garden. Native plants featured. Exhibits.

MARIE SELBY BOTANICAL GARDEN: 811 South Palm Avenue, Sarasota, 34236, (941)366-5731. Wonderful demonstration garden for both butterflies and native plants.

SOURCES & RESOURCES

Association of Florida Native Nurseries
P. O. Box 434
Melrose, FL 32666-0434
www.afnn.org
This trade organization publishes an extremely useful annual directory of member nurseries that also lists the plants they have available.

Association of Tropical Lepidopterists
1717 NW 45th Avenue
Gainesville, FL 32605
www.troplep.org
Newsletter with membership. Journal also available at additional cost.

Butterfly Seed Farms
P. O. Box 1546
Manchaca, TX 78652-1546
www.butterflyseeds.com
Send $1.00 and address for catalog.

Earthly Goods Ltd.
P. O. Box 614
New Albany, IN 47150
www.earthlygoods.com
Free catalog, order online

Florida Federation of Garden Clubs
1400 S Denning Drive
Winter Park, FL 32789
(407)647-7016
www.ffgc.org
Has state and district butterfly garden coordinators. Very active in installing school butterfly gardens. Butterfly sanctuary certification program (application at website).

Florida Native Plant Society
P. O. Box 690278
Vero Beach, FL 32969-0278
(561)562-1598
www.fnps.org
Local chapters statewide, excellent newsletters, information, plant sources, monthly field trips.

Florida Wildlife Extension
Florida Cooperative Extension Service
University of Florida
P. O. Box 110430
Gainesville, FL 32611-0430
(352)846-0554
www.wec.ufl.edu/extension
Local offices statewide. Lots of free information, booklets, brochures. Florida Wildlife Habitat Program Yard certification.

Florida Yards & Neighborhoods Program
University of Florida
P. O. Box 110670
Gainesville, FL 32611
hort.ufl.edu/fyn
"Certified Florida Yard" program, free publications and information.

Lady Bird Johnson Wildflower Center
4801 LaCrosse Avenue
Austin, TX 78739-1702
(512)292-4200
www.wildflower.org
This nonprofit educational organization was founded in 1982 to teach people about the environmental necessity, economic value and natural beauty of native plants.

Mail-Order Natives
P. O. Box 9366
Lee, Fl 32059
(850)973-4688
monnatives@aol.com
Lots of Florida natives, with some other plants also available. View catalog online, or send $2.00 and SASE

North American Butterfly Association
4 Delaware Road
Morristown, NJ 07960
www.naba.org
American Butterflies magazine and butterfly gardening newsletter with membership.

WildSeed Farms
P. O. Box 3000
Fredricksburg, Tx 78624-3000
(800)848-0078
www.wildseedfarms.com
Free catalog of wildflower and herb seeds. Most can be purchased either by the packet, ounce or pound.

The Xerces Society
10 SW Ash Street
Portland, OR 97204
www.xerces.org
Non-profit organization focused on the preservation of butterfly habitat as well as that of other invertebrates.

QUICK REFERENCE CHART

SCIENTIFIC NAME	COMMON NAME	PLANT TYPE	TYPICAL HEIGHT
Amorpha frutescens	False indigobush	S	12'
Amyris spp.	Torchwood	S/T	15'
Anethum graveolens	Dill	A	4'
Aristolochia grandiflora	Pelican flower	V	-
Aristolochia maxima	Dutchman's pipe	V	-
Aristolochia pentandra	Marsh's Dutchman's pipe	V	-
Aristolochia serpentaria	Virginia snakeroot	P	1'
Aristolochia tomentosa	Woolly pipevine	V	-
Asclepias curassavica	Scarlet milkweed	P	4'
Asclepias humistrata	Sandhill milkweed	P	3'
Asclepias incarnata	Pink swamp milkweed	P	3'
Asclepias perennis	White swamp milkweed	P	2'
Asclepias tomentosa	Velvetleaf milkweed	P	2'
Asclepias tuberosa	Butterfly-weed	P	1'-2'
Asclepias verticillata	Whorled milkweed	P	2'
Asclepias viridis	Green-crowned milkweed	P	2'
Asimina angustifolia	Narrow-leaf mawpaw	S	4'+
Asimina obovata	Bigflower/flag pawpaw	S	12'+
Asimina parviflora	Smallflower pawpaw	T	15'
Asimina reticulata	Flatwoods pawpaw	S	4'+
Asimina triloba	Common pawpaw	S/T	35'+
Aster carolinianus	Climbing aster	V/S	8'
Aster dumosus	Bushy aster	P	3'+
Aster elliottii	Elliott's aster	P	3'
Bacopa caroliniana	Lemon bacopa	Q	4"
Bacopa monnieri	Water hyssop	Q	4"
Boehmeria cylindrica	False nettle	P	2'+
Buddleia spp.	Butterfly bush	S	10'+
Carphephorus corymbosus	Florida paintbrush	P	3'
Carphephorus odoratissimus	Vanilla plant	P	3'

118

SOIL TYPE	DROUGHT TOLERANCE	LIGHT REQ.	FLOWER COLOR	BLOOM TIME	USED FOR	FLORIDA ZONES
L-O	L	P	U	Sp-Su	L, N	N, C
S-L	H	P-F	W	Y	L	S
L-O	L	P-F	Y	Sp	L	N, C, S
S-O	M	P-F	R/W	Su	L	C, S
S-O	M	P-F	U/W	Su	L	C, S
S-O	M	P-F	G/U	Y	L	S
S-O	M	P-F	G	Sp	L	N, C
L-O	L	P-F	Y/U	Sp	L	N
S-O	H	P-F	R/Y/O	Sp-F	L, N	N, C, S
S	H	F	W	Sp-Su	L, N	N, C, S
L-O	L	F	P	S	L, N	N, C, S
L-O	M	P-F	W	Sp-F	L, N	N, C
S	H	F	G	Sp-F	L, N	N, C, S
S	H	F	R, O, Y	Su	L, N	N, C, S
S	H	F	G	Sp-F	L, N	C
L-O	M	P-F	Y-G	Sp	L, N	N, C, S
S	H	P-F	W	Sp-Su	L	N, C
S	H	F	W	Sp	L	N, C, S
L-O	L	P	R	Sp	L	N, C
S	H	P-F	W	Sp	L	N, C, S
O	M	P	R	Sp	L	N, C
O	M	P-F	U	F-W	N	N, C, S
S-L	M	P-F	B	Su-F	N	N, C, S
L-O	L	F	P	Su-F	N	N, C, S
O	L	F	B	Su-F	L	N, C, S
O	L	F	W	Su-F	L	N, C, S
O	L	P	G	Sp-F	L	N, C, S
L-O	M	F	var.	Sp-F	N	N, C
S	H	F	L	F	N	N, C, S
L-O	L	M	P-L	F-W	N	N, C, S

QUICK REFERENCE CHART *(continued)*

SCIENTIFIC NAME	COMMON NAME	PLANT TYPE	TYPICAL HEIGHT
Carphephorus paniculatus	Deer-tongue	P	3'
Centrosema virginianum	Butterfly pea	V	-
Cephalanthus occidentalis	Buttonbush	S	10'+
Chamaecrista fasciculata	Partridge pea	A	2'+
Chrysopsis scabrella	Goldenaster	B	3'
Conoclinum coelestinum	Mistflower	P	2'+
Coreopsis leavenworthii	Tickseed	P	3'+
Coreopsis nudata	Swamp coreopsis	A/P	2'
Duranta repens	Golden dewdrop	S	18'+
Dyschoriste oblongifolia	Twinflower	P	8"
Echinacea purpurea	Purple coneflower	P	2'+
Elephantopus elatus	Elephant's foot	P	1'-2'
Eupatorium fistulosum	Joe-pye-weed	P	10'+
Euthamia caroliniana	Flat-topped goldenrod	P	3'
Foeniculum vulgare	Fennel	A	5'
Gaillardia pulchella	Blanketflower	A	1'
Garberia heterophylla	Garberia	S	6'
Glandularia maritima	Beach verbena	P	?
Glandularia tampensis	Tampa verbena	P	1'+
Gnaphalium spp.	Cudweed	A	1'
Hamelia patens	Firebush	S	10'+
Helianthus angustifolius	Swamp sunflower	P	6'
Helianthus debilis	Beach sunflower	A/P	2'
Heliotropium angiospermum	Scorpion Tail	P	3'
Heliotropium currasavicum	Seaside heliotrope	P	1'+
Ipomopsis rubra	Standingcypress	A/B	3'
Justicia spp.	Water willow	P	1'
Lachnanthes caroliniana	Redroot	P	1-3'
Lantana canescens	Hammock shrubverbena	S	3'
Lantana depressa var. *depressa*	Rockland shrubverbena	S	3'

SOIL TYPE	DROUGHT TOLERANCE	LIGHT REQ.	FLOWER COLOR	BLOOM TIME	USED FOR	FLORIDA ZONES
S-L	H	P-F	P-U	F-W	N	N, C, S
S-O	H	F	P	Sp-F	L	N, C, S
O	L	F	W	Su-F	N	N, C, S
S	H	F	Y	Y	L	N, C, S
S	H	F	Y	Su-F	N	N, C, S
L, O	L	P-F	B-U	Y	N	N, C, S
S-O	M	F	Y	Y	N	N, C, S
L-O	L	P-F	P	Sp	N	N
O	H	F	L	Su-F	N	C, S
S	H	P-F	L-B	Sp-F	L, N	N, C, S
S-L	M	F	P-U	Sp-Su	N	N, C
S-L	M	P-F	U	Su-F	N	N, C, S
L-O	M	F	P-U	S	N	N, C
S-L	H	F	Y	F	N	N, C, S
L-O	M	P-F	Y	Sp	L	N, C, S
S	H	F	R, Y	Y	N	N, C, S
S	H	F	P	F	N	C, S
S	H	F	P-L	Y	N	S
S	M	P-F	L	Y	N	N, C, S
S	H	F	W	Y	L	N, C, S
S-O	H	P-F	O/R	Y	N	C, S
L-O	L	F	Y	S-F	N	N, C
S-L	H	F	Y	Y	N	N, C, S
S	H	F	W	Y	N	C, S
S	H	F	W	Y	N	C, S
S	H	F	R	S-F	N	N, C
L-O	L	P-F	P	Sp-F	L	N, C, S
L-O	M	F	W	Sp-F	N	N, C, S
S	H	F	W	Y	N	S
S	H	F	Y	Y	N	S

121

QUICK REFERENCE CHART (continued)

SCIENTIFIC NAME	COMMON NAME	PLANT TYPE	TYPICAL HEIGHT
Lantana depressa var. *floridana*	Sanibel shrubverbena	S	3'
Lantana depressa var. *sanibelensis*	Sanibel shrubverbena	S	3'
Lantana involucrata	Wild (button) sage	S	15'+
Lantana montevidensis	Weeping lantana	S	1'
Liatris chapmanii	Chapman's blazing star	P	2'+
Liatris gracilis	Slender blazing star	P	3'
Liatris spicata	Dense blazing btar	P	3'+
Liatris tenuifolia	Shortleaf blazing star	P	4'
Lindera benzoin	Spicebush	S	8'
Liriodendron tulipifera	Tulip poplar	T	75'+
Lobelia cardinalis	Cardinal flower	P	4'+
Magnolia virginiana	Sweet bay	T	50'
Monarda punctata	Dotted horsemint	P	3'+
Passiflora incarnata	Maypop	V	-
Passiflora lutea	Yellow passionvine	V	-
Passiflora suberosa	Corky-stemmed passionvine	V	-
Pentas lanceolata	Pentas	S	1-4'
Persea borbonia	Red bay	T	50'+
Persea borbonia var. *humilis*	Silk bay	T	30'
Persea palustris	Swamp bay	T	30'
Petroselinum crispum	Parsley	B	1'
Phlox drummondii	Garden phlox	A	1'
Phlox nivalis	Trailing phlox	P	8"
Phlox pilosa	Downy phlox	P	2'
Physostegia purpurea	False dragonhead	P	3'
Piloblephis rigida	Pennyroyal	P	8"
Pityopsis graminifolia	Narrowleaf silkgrass	P	1'
Pontederia cordata	Pickerelweed	Q	3'
Prunus serotina	Black cherry	T	50'+
Rhododendron austrinum	Florida flame azalea	S	15'

SOIL TYPE	DROUGHT TOLERANCE	LIGHT REQ.	FLOWER COLOR	BLOOM TIME	USED FOR	FLORIDA ZONES
S	H	F	Y	Y	N	C, S
S	H	F	Y	Y	N	C, S
S	H	F	W	Sp-F	N	C, S
S	H	P-F	L	Sp-F	N	N, C, S
S	H	F	L	Su-F	N	N, C, S
S	H	P-F	L	Su-F	N	N, C
S-L	M	F	L	Su-F	N	N, C
S	H	F	L	F	N	N, C
L-O	M	P-F	Y	Sp	L	N
L-O	M	F	G/O	Sp	L	N, C
L-O	L	P-F	R	Su-F	N	N, C
L-O	M	P-F	W	S	L	N, C, S
S-L	M	F	P/U	Su-F	N	N, C
S-O	H	F	U	Su-F	L	N, C, S
S	H	S-F	Y-G	Su	L	S
S	H	S-F	Y-G	Y	L	N, C
S-O	M	P-F	var.	Y	N	N, C, S
S-O	M	P-F	Y	Sp	L	N, C, S
S	H	F	Y	Sp	L	C, S
O	L	P-F	Y	Sp	L	N, C, S
L-O	L	P-F	Y	Sp	L	N, C, S
S-O	M	F	var.	Sp-Su	N	N, C
S	H	P-F	P	Sp-Su	N	N, C
S	H	P-F	P	Sp-Su	N	N, C
O	L	P-F	U	Sp-F	N	N, C, S
S	H	F	L	Sp-Su	N	N, C, S
S	H	F	Y	F	N	N, C, S
L-O	L	F	B	Sp-F	N	N, C, S
O	M	P-F	W	Sp	L, N	N, C
L-O	M	P-S	Y/O	Sp	N	N, C

QUICK REFERENCE CHART *(continued)*

SCIENTIFIC NAME	COMMON NAME	PLANT TYPE	TYPICAL HEIGHT
Rudbeckia hirta	Black-eyed susan	A/B/P	2'
Ruellia caroliniensis	Ruellia	P	1'
Salvia coccinea	Tropical sage	A	4'+
Sarcostemma clausum	White vine	V	—
Salvia lyrata	Lyre-leaved sage	A	1'+
Sassafras albidum	Sassafras	S	15'+
Senna ligustrina	Privet cassia	S	6'
Senna mexicana var. *chapmanii*	Bahama cassia	S/T	12'+
Solidago fistulosa	Pinebarren goldenrod	P	6'
Solidago odora var. *chapmanii*	Chapman's goldenrod	P	3'+
Solidago sempervirens	Seaside goldenrod	P	6'+
Solidago stricta	Wand goldenrod	P	4'+
Stachytarpheta jamaicensis	Trailing blue porterweed	S	1'+
Stokesia laevis	Stokes' aster	P	1'+
Vernonia angustifolia	Tall ironweed	P	3'
Vernonia gigantea	Giant ironweed	P	6'+
Wisteria frutescens	American wisteria	V	-
Zamia pumila	Coontie	S	1'-2'
Zanthoxylum clava-herculis	Hercules' Club	T	15'+
Zanthoxylum fagara	Wild Lime	T	25'+

KEY:

Plant type: T=tree, S=shrub, V=vine, A=annual wildflower, B=biennial wildflower, P=perennial wildflower, Q=aquatic plant

Soil type: O=organic, L=loamy, S=sandy

Drought tolerance: L=low, M=medium, H=high

Light: F=full sun, P=partial shade, S=Shade

Flower color: B=blue, G=green, L=lavender, O=orange, P=pink, U=purple, R=red, W=white, Y=yellow

Bloom time: W=winter, Sp=spring, Su=summer, F=fall, Y=year-round

Dormant period: W=winter, Sp=spring, Su=summer, F=fall

Used for: L=larval food, N=nectar

Zones: N=north Florida, C=central Florida, S=south Florida

SOIL TYPE	DROUGHT TOLERANCE	LIGHT REQ.	FLOWER COLOR	BLOOM TIME	USED FOR	FLORIDA ZONES
S-O	M	F	Y	Su-F	N	N, C, S
S-O	H	P-F	L	Y	L, N	N, C, S
S	H	F	R	Y	N	N, C, S
S–L	H	P	W	Y	L, N	C, S
S-O	H	P-F	B	Sp-F	N	N, C, S
S-O	M	P-F	G/Y	Sp	L	N, C
S	H	P-F	Y	Y	L	C, S
S	H	P-F	Y	Sp-Su	L	C, S
S-O	H	P-F	Y	F	N	N, C, S
S	H	P-F	Y	Sp-F	N	N, C, S
S	M	F	Y	Y	N	N, C, S
S	M	F	Y	Su-F	N	N, C, S
S-L	H	F	B	Y	N	C, S
S-O	L	P-F	L	Sp-Su	N	N, C
S	H	F	U	Su-F	N	N, C
S	M	F	U	Su-F	N	N, C
L-O	L	F	U	Sp	L	N, C
S	H	P-F	-	-	L	C, S
S	H	P-F	W	Sp-Su	L	C, S
S-O	H	F	Y-G	Sp-Su	L, N	C, S

BIBLIOGRAPHY

Ajilvsgi, Geyata. 1990. *Butterfly Gardening for the South.* Dallas, TX: Taylor Publishing Co.

Austin, Daniel A. 1991. *Coastal Dune Plants: The Common Wildflowers, Trees, Shrubs & Vines of Southeast Florida's Ocean-Side Communities.* Boca Raton, FL: Gumbo Limbo Nature Center of South Palm Beach County, Inc.

Austin, Daniel A. 1997. *Coastal Hammock & Mangrove Guide: The Native Trees, Shrubs, & Vines of S.E. Florida's Hammock and Mangrove Communities.* Boca Raton, FL: Gumbo Limbo Nature Center of South Palm Beach County, Inc.

Austin, Daniel A. 1993. *Scrub Plant Guide: A Pocket Guide to the Common Plants of Southern Florida's Scrub Community.* Boca Raton, FL: Gumbo Limbo Nature Center of South Palm Beach County, Inc.

Baker, Mary Francis. 1938. *Florida Wild Flowers: An Introduction to the Florida Flora.* New York: Macmillan.

Bell, C. Ritchie and Bryan J. Taylor. 1982. *Florida Wildflowers and Roadside Plants.* Chapel Hill, N.C.: Laurel Hill Press.

Broschat, Timothy K. and Alan W. Meerow. 1991. *Betrock's Reference Guide to Florida Landscape Plants.* Hollywood, FL: Betrock Information Systems, Inc.

Chaplin, Lois Trigg and Monica Moran Brandies. 1998. *The Florida Gardener's Book of Lists.* Dallas, TX: Taylor Publishing Co.

Emmel, Thomas C., and Brian Kinney. 1997. *Florida's Fabulous Butterflies.* Tampa, FL: World Publications.

Fleming, Glenn. 1979. *Wild Flowers of Florida.* Miami, FL: Banyan Books, Inc.

Florida Division of Forestry. 1985. *Forest Trees of Florida (16th Ed.).* Gainesville, FL: Florida Forestry Association.

Gerberg, Eugene J. and Ross H. Arnett, Jr. 1989. *Florida Butterflies.* Baltimore, MD: Natural Science Publications.

Glassberg, Jeffrey, Marc C. Minno and John V. Calhoun. *Butterflies through Binoculars: A Field, Finding and Gardening Guide to Butterflies in Florida.* 2000. New York: Oxford University Press.

Huegel, Craig. 1991. *Butterfly Gardening with Florida's Native Plants.* Orlando, FL: Florida Native Plant Society.

Huegel, Craig. 1995. *Florida Plants for Wildlife: A Selection Guide to Native Trees and Shrubs.* Orlando, FL: Florida Native Plant Society.

Jameson, Michael and Richard Moyroud (Editors). 1991. *Xeric Landscaping with Florida Native Plants.* San Antonio, FL: Assoc. of Florida Native Nurseries.

Long, Robert W. and Olga Lakela. 1971. *A Flora of Tropical Florida: A Manual of the Seed Plants and Ferns of Southern Peninsular Florida.* Coral Gables, FL: University of Miami Press.

MacCubbin, Tom. 1997. *Florida Home Grown.* Winter Park, FL: Waterview Press.

Minno, Marc C. and Maria Minno. 1999. *Florida Butterfly Gardening: A Complete Guide to Attracting, Identifying and Enjoying Butterflies of the Lower South.* Gainesville, FL: University Press of Florida.

Nellis, David W. 1994. *Seashore Plants of South Florida and the Caribbean.* Sarasota, FL: Pineapple Press, Inc.

Nelson, Gil. 1994. *The Trees of Florida.* Sarasota, FL: Pineapple Press, Inc.

Opler, Paul A. 1992. *A Field Guide to Eastern Butterflies.* New York: Houghton Mifflin Co.

Peebles, Diane. Undated. *50 Native Trees of Pinellas County: A Pictorial Identification Guide.* Tarpon Springs, FL: Anderson Environmental Education Center, Pinellas County Park Department.

Phillips, Harry R. 1985. *Growing and Propagating Wild Flowers.* Chapel Hill, NC: University of North Carolina Press.

Pyle, Robert Michael. 1995. *National Audubon Society Field Guide to North American Butterflies.* New York: Alfred A. Knopf.

Satterthwaithe, Loretta N. and Robert H. Stamps (Editors). 1994. *Common Native Plants of Central Florida.* Orlando, FL: Tarflower Chapter, Florida Native Plant Society.

Schaefer, Joe, Craig N. Huegel and Frank J. Mazzotti. 1990. *Butterfly Gardening in Florida.* Gainesville, FL: Document WEC-21 of the Wildlife Ecology and Conservation department, Florida Cooperative Extension Service, Institute of Food and Agricultural Sciences, University of Florida.

Schaefer, Joe and George Tanner. 1998. *Landscaping for Florida's Wildlife: Re-creating Native Ecosystems in Your Yard.* Gainesville, FL: University Press of Florida.

Stokes, Donald and Lillian with Ernest Williams. 1991. *The Butterfly Book.* Boston, MA: Little, Brown and Company.

Stresau, Frederic B. 1986. *Florida, My Eden.* Port Salerno, FL: Florida Classics Library.

Suncoast Native Plant Society. 1997. *The Right Plants for Dry Places: Native Plant Landscaping in Central Florida.* St. Petersburg, FL: Great Outdoors Publishing Co.

Tasker, Georgia. 1984. *Wild Things: The Return of Native Plants.* Winter Park, FL: Florida Native Plant Society.

Taylor, Walter Kingsley. 1998. *Florida Wildflowers in their Natural Communities.* Gainesville, FL: University Press of Florida.

Taylor, Walter Kingsley. 1992. *Guide to Florida Wildflowers.* Dallas, TX: Taylor Publishing Company.

Wasowski, Sally and Andy Wasowski. 1994. *Gardening with Native Plants of the South.* Dallas, TX: Taylor Publishing Company.

Watkins, John V. and Sheehan, Thomas J. 1975. *Florida Landscape Plants, Native and Exotic.* (Revised edition). Gainesville, FL: University Presses of Florida.

Wright, Amy Bartlett. 1993. *Peterson First Guide to Caterpillars of North America.* New York: Houghton Mifflin Co.

Wunderlin, Richard P. 1998. *Guide to the Vascular Plants of Florida.* Gainesville, FL: University Press of Florida.

Yarlett, Lewis L. 1997. *Common Grasses of Florida and the Southeast.* Orlando, FL: Florida Native Plant Society.

INDEX

About the Author

Pamela F. Traas is a freelance writer, photographer and butterfly enthusiast. She has been a contributing editor and columnist for the *Tropical Breeze* newspaper and has had articles and photographs published in the *Tampa Tribune* and *St. Petersburg Times* newspapers, *Florida Gardening* and *Guideposts for Kids* magazines, and many other publications. Pam's formative years were spent raising tadpoles on a small lake in Orlando called Lake Barton. From there she moved to Satellite Beach in the early 1960s. Pam now enjoys watching butterflies in her garden in Safety Harbor, Florida with her husband, daughter, and dog Floppy.